RED TEAM OPERATIONS ATTACK

BLACK BOX HACKING, SOCIAL ENGINEERING & WEB APP SCANNING

4 BOOKS IN 1

BOOK 1
RED TEAM ESSENTIALS: A BEGINNER'S GUIDE TO ATTACK STRATEGIES

BOOK 2
UNLOCKING THE BLACK BOX: ADVANCED TECHNIQUES IN ETHICAL HACKING

BOOK 3
MASTERING THE ART OF SOCIAL ENGINEERING: TACTICS FOR RED TEAM PROFESSIONALS

BOOK 4
WEB APP SCANNING MASTERY: EXPERT TECHNIQUES FOR RED TEAM SPECIALISTS

ROB BOTWRIGHT

Published by Rob Botwright
Library of Congress Cataloging-in-Publication Data
ISBN 978-1-83938-558-2
Cover design by Rizzo

Disclaimer

The contents of this book are based on extensive research and the best available historical sources. However, the author and publisher make no claims, promises, or guarantees about the accuracy, completeness, or adequacy of the information contained herein. The information in this book is provided on an "as is" basis, and the author and publisher disclaim any and all liability for any errors, omissions, or inaccuracies in the information or for any actions taken in reliance on such information. The opinions and views expressed in this book are those of the author and do not necessarily reflect the official policy or position of any organization or individual mentioned in this book. Any reference to specific people, places, or events is intended only to provide historical context and is not intended to defame or malign any group, individual, or entity. The information in this book is intended for educational and entertainment purposes only. It is not intended to be a substitute for professional advice or judgment. Readers are encouraged to conduct their own research and to seek professional advice where appropriate. Every effort has been made to obtain necessary permissions and acknowledgments for all images and other copyrighted material used in this book. Any errors or omissions in this regard are unintentional, and the author and publisher will correct them in future editions.

TABLE OF CONTENTS – BOOK 1 - RED TEAM ESSENTIALS: A BEGINNER'S GUIDE TO ATTACK STRATEGIES

Introduction 5
Chapter 1: Understanding Red Teaming 8
Chapter 2: The Fundamentals of Cybersecurity 14
Chapter 3: Reconnaissance and Information Gathering 21
Chapter 4: Vulnerability Assessment and Scanning 27
Chapter 5: Exploiting Common System Weaknesses 34
Chapter 6: Password Cracking and Authentication Attacks 42
Chapter 7: Social Engineering Techniques 49
Chapter 8: Malware and Payload Delivery 56
Chapter 9: Evading Detection and Covering Tracks 63
Chapter 10: Reporting and Post-Attack Analysis 70

TABLE OF CONTENTS – BOOK 2 - UNLOCKING THE BLACK BOX: ADVANCED TECHNIQUES IN ETHICAL HACKING

Chapter 1: Advanced Hacking Methodologies 79
Chapter 2: Cryptography and Secure Communications 87
Chapter 3: Exploiting Zero-Day Vulnerabilities 95
Chapter 4: Advanced Network Scanning and Enumeration 102
Chapter 5: Privilege Escalation and Post-Exploitation 109
Chapter 6: Advanced Web Application Attacks 115
Chapter 7: Wireless and IoT Hacking 122
Chapter 8: Evading Advanced Security Measures 129
Chapter 9: Advanced Social Engineering Tactics 136
Chapter 10: Legal and Ethical Considerations in Ethical Hacking 142

TABLE OF CONTENTS – BOOK 3 - MASTERING THE ART OF SOCIAL ENGINEERING: TACTICS FOR RED TEAM PROFESSIONALS

Chapter 1: The Psychology of Social Engineering 150
Chapter 2: Building Effective Pretexting Scenarios 158
Chapter 3: Impersonation and Identity Spoofing 167
Chapter 4: Manipulating Human Behavior 176
Chapter 5: Phishing and Spear Phishing Attacks 183
Chapter 6: Physical Security Exploits 190
Chapter 7: Psychological Manipulation in Social Engineering 196
Chapter 8: Advanced Social Engineering Techniques 203
Chapter 9: Social Engineering in Red Team Operations 210
Chapter 10: Mitigating Social Engineering Threats 217

TABLE OF CONTENTS – BOOK 4 - WEB APP SCANNING MASTERY: EXPERT TECHNIQUES FOR RED TEAM SPECIALISTS

Chapter 1: Fundamentals of Web Application Security 225
Chapter 2: Advanced Web App Reconnaissance 231
Chapter 3: In-Depth Web App Scanning Tools 239
Chapter 4: Automated Vulnerability Assessment 247
Chapter 5: Manual Testing and Exploitation 256
Chapter 6: API Security Testing 264
Chapter 7: Web Application Firewalls (WAFs) Bypass Techniques 274
Chapter 8: Exploiting Common Web App Vulnerabilities 280
Chapter 9: Advanced Session Management and Authentication Attacks 287
Chapter 10: Reporting and Remediation in Web App Scanning 291
Conclusion 299

Introduction

Welcome to the world of cybersecurity, where the battle between defenders and adversaries unfolds in the digital realm. In this era of constant connectivity, the importance of safeguarding sensitive information, critical infrastructure, and personal privacy cannot be overstated. To protect against evolving threats, organizations and individuals alike turn to the expertise of skilled professionals known as "red teamers" and ethical hackers who employ a variety of strategies to identify vulnerabilities before malicious actors do.

In this exclusive book bundle, "Red Team Operations: Attack," we embark on a journey into the intricate world of red teaming, ethical hacking, social engineering, and web application security. Comprising four meticulously crafted volumes, this collection is designed to provide both aspiring and seasoned cybersecurity enthusiasts with a comprehensive guide to mastering the art of digital warfare.

Book 1 - Red Team Essentials: A Beginner's Guide to Attack Strategies In our first book, we lay the groundwork for understanding the fundamentals of red teaming. Designed for beginners, this volume delves into the critical aspects of planning, reconnaissance, and attack methodologies. We explore the mindset required to emulate adversaries effectively and provide insights into the techniques used to assess and fortify an organization's security defenses.

Book 2 - Unlocking the Black Box: Advanced Techniques in Ethical Hacking Building on the foundational knowledge acquired in the first book, we venture into the realm of advanced ethical hacking in our second installment. Readers will explore advanced penetration testing and vulnerability assessment techniques, equipping them with the skills needed to uncover hidden weaknesses within systems and applications.

Book 3 - Mastering the Art of Social Engineering: Tactics for Red Team Professionals In our third book, we shift our focus to the human element of security. Here, we delve deep into the psychology behind social engineering, the art of manipulating individuals to gain unauthorized access. This volume equips readers with a robust understanding of the tactics employed by red team professionals to raise awareness and protect against social engineering attacks.

Book 4 - Web App Scanning Mastery: Expert Techniques for Red Team Specialists Our final book completes the comprehensive journey by delving into the intricacies of web application security. Readers will master the art of scanning and vulnerability assessment, gain an understanding of API authentication, and learn techniques for evading Web Application Firewall (WAF) detection. Expertly securing web applications is vital in today's cybersecurity landscape, and this volume provides the knowledge needed to excel in this critical area.

As we embark on this exploration of "Red Team Operations: Attack," we invite you to immerse yourself in the world of ethical hacking, penetration testing, and cybersecurity strategy. Whether you are new to the field or a seasoned professional seeking to expand your skill set, this book bundle offers a comprehensive roadmap to becoming a proficient and responsible guardian of the digital realm. Join us on this educational journey, and let's explore the fascinating world of cyber warfare together.

BOOK 1
RED TEAM ESSENTIALS
A BEGINNER'S GUIDE TO ATTACK STRATEGIES

ROB BOTWRIGHT

Chapter 1: Understanding Red Teaming

In the world of cybersecurity, understanding the objectives and goals of red teaming is paramount. Red teaming is a strategic and systematic approach to assessing the security of an organization's systems, processes, and defenses. It's not just about trying to breach systems; rather, it's a comprehensive examination of an organization's security posture. The primary goal of red teaming is to simulate real-world attacks and identify vulnerabilities before malicious hackers can exploit them.

By taking on the role of the adversary, red teams aim to uncover weaknesses in an organization's security infrastructure and provide actionable insights for improvement. This process is not adversarial in nature; instead, it is a collaborative effort aimed at enhancing an organization's overall security resilience. Red teams work closely with the organization's blue teams, which are responsible for defending against cyber threats, to create a robust security ecosystem.

One key objective of red teaming is to identify and test critical assets and systems that could be attractive targets for attackers. These assets may include sensitive data, customer information, financial systems, and more. By focusing on these high-value targets, red teams help organizations prioritize their security efforts and allocate resources effectively.

Another critical objective of red teaming is to assess an organization's incident response and detection capabilities. Red team exercises often involve various tactics, techniques, and procedures (TTPs) commonly used by real adversaries. This allows organizations to evaluate their ability to detect and respond to different types of cyberattacks promptly.

Additionally, red teaming helps organizations evaluate their security awareness and training programs. It assesses how well employees can identify and respond to social engineering attempts, phishing attacks, and other forms of manipulation.

One of the essential aspects of red teaming is the emulation of real-world attack scenarios. This means that red teams must stay up-to-date with the latest hacking techniques, vulnerabilities, and threat actor behaviors. They need to adapt and evolve their tactics to mirror the ever-changing threat landscape accurately. This ensures that the assessments conducted by red teams remain relevant and effective.

It's important to note that red teaming is not a one-size-fits-all approach. The specific objectives and goals of a red team engagement can vary depending on the organization's industry, size, and unique security challenges. For example, a financial institution may have different priorities compared to a healthcare organization, and a red team engagement would be tailored accordingly.

One common misconception is that red teaming is solely focused on technology and infrastructure. While assessing technical vulnerabilities is a significant part of the process, red teams also examine the human element of security. Social engineering, insider threats, and physical security are all areas that can be assessed to uncover weaknesses.

Ultimately, the primary goal of red teaming is to improve an organization's overall security posture. It achieves this by providing a holistic view of the organization's strengths and weaknesses, both in terms of technology and human factors. Red team findings are used to drive improvements in security policies, procedures, and technologies, making the organization more resilient to cyber threats.

In summary, red teaming plays a crucial role in modern cybersecurity by simulating real-world attacks and helping organizations identify and address vulnerabilities effectively. Its objectives and goals encompass a wide range of security aspects, from technical weaknesses to human factors, with the ultimate aim of enhancing an organization's overall security posture in an ever-evolving threat landscape.

To truly understand the world of red teaming, it's essential to explore its historical roots and how it has evolved over time. Red teaming, as a concept, has its origins in military strategy and war gaming. It can be traced back to ancient civilizations where military leaders would employ independent groups to simulate opposing forces, allowing them to test their strategies and tactics.

One of the earliest recorded instances of red teaming can be found in the writings of the Chinese military strategist Sun Tzu, who lived in the 6th century BC. Sun Tzu's "The Art of War" emphasizes the importance of understanding the enemy's mindset and tactics to achieve victory. This ancient wisdom laid the groundwork for the principles of red teaming we see today.

Moving forward in history, red teaming gained prominence during the Cold War era. In the United States, the concept was employed by the military and intelligence agencies to assess vulnerabilities and weaknesses in their defense systems. The term "red team" was used to refer to the simulated adversary, often representing the Soviet Union or other potential threats. These red teams conducted exercises to test the readiness of U.S. forces and identify areas that required improvement.

During this period, red teaming expanded beyond the military and found applications in other sectors, including government agencies and private organizations. The practice of challenging assumptions and identifying vulnerabilities through simulation became valuable not only in defense but also in areas such as risk management and business strategy.

As the digital age dawned, the concept of red teaming adapted to address the growing threat of cyberattacks. Red teams began to focus on assessing the security of computer systems and networks. This shift in focus led to the emergence of the field of cybersecurity red teaming, which is now a critical component of modern security practices.

Today, red teaming is not limited to military or governmental organizations; it is widely employed across various industries and sectors. Organizations recognize the need to proactively assess their security posture and readiness against a diverse range of threats. Red team engagements are now common in financial institutions, healthcare organizations, technology companies, and many others.

In the context of cybersecurity, red teaming has become an essential tool for identifying and mitigating vulnerabilities in an organization's digital infrastructure. Red teams simulate real-world cyberattacks, employing tactics, techniques, and procedures (TTPs) that mirror those of actual threat actors. This enables organizations to evaluate their defenses and incident response capabilities effectively.

One of the key benefits of red teaming is its ability to provide a holistic view of an organization's security posture. It goes beyond simply scanning for technical vulnerabilities. Red teams assess the human element of security, including the effectiveness of security awareness programs and the susceptibility of employees to social engineering attacks.

Moreover, red teaming often uncovers systemic weaknesses in an organization's policies, procedures, and processes. It highlights areas where improvements are needed, not only in technology but also in governance and compliance.

In recent years, red teaming has also embraced the concept of "purple teaming." Purple teaming is a collaborative approach that brings together red teams (the attackers) and blue teams (the defenders) to work closely in assessing and improving an organization's security. This collaboration fosters a better understanding of the evolving threat landscape and enables organizations to fine-tune their defenses more effectively.

In summary, the historical perspective on red teaming reveals its roots in military strategy and its evolution into a vital practice in cybersecurity and risk management. It has grown from its origins in warfare simulations to become a multidisciplinary approach for assessing and enhancing the security posture of organizations in an ever-changing and increasingly digital world.

Chapter 2: The Fundamentals of Cybersecurity

Understanding the principles of information security is fundamental in today's interconnected world. These principles provide a solid foundation for protecting sensitive data, systems, and networks from various threats and vulnerabilities. At the core of information security is the principle of confidentiality, which ensures that data is accessible only to authorized individuals or systems.

Confidentiality is about maintaining the privacy of information, preventing unauthorized access, and safeguarding sensitive data from falling into the wrong hands. It involves implementing access controls, encryption, and other measures to keep information confidential.

Another critical principle is integrity, which focuses on the accuracy and reliability of data. Integrity ensures that data remains unchanged and uncorrupted during storage, transmission, and processing. Data integrity measures include data validation, checksums, and digital signatures.

Availability is the third cornerstone of information security. It ensures that data and resources are readily available to authorized users when needed. Availability safeguards against disruptions, such as denial-of-service attacks or system failures, that can impact an organization's ability to function.

Authentication is a principle that verifies the identity of users or systems, ensuring that they are who they claim to be. Strong authentication methods, such as two-factor authentication (2FA) and biometrics, enhance security by preventing unauthorized access.

Authorization complements authentication by determining what authorized users or systems are allowed to do once they gain access. It involves setting permissions and access controls to restrict actions and privileges to specific roles or individuals.

Accountability is the principle of traceability, which allows organizations to track and audit the actions of users and systems. Accountability is crucial for identifying security incidents, understanding the impact of breaches, and holding individuals or entities responsible for their actions. The principle of non-repudiation ensures that parties cannot deny their involvement in a transaction or the authenticity of a message. Digital signatures and transaction logs are common mechanisms used to establish non-repudiation.

Risk management is a core principle that involves identifying, assessing, and mitigating risks to an organization's information assets. It requires a proactive approach to understand potential threats and vulnerabilities and implement controls to reduce the associated risks.

Security policies and procedures are essential for guiding security practices within an organization. They outline the rules, guidelines, and standards that employees and stakeholders must follow to ensure information security.

Training and awareness are crucial to maintaining effective information security. Employees and users should be educated about security best practices, threats, and how to respond to security incidents.

Incident response is a principle that focuses on how an organization reacts to security incidents when they occur. It involves having a well-defined plan in place to detect, contain, mitigate, and recover from security breaches.

The principle of defense in depth emphasizes the importance of layering security controls to create multiple barriers against threats. This approach makes it more challenging for attackers to breach an organization's defenses.

Security by design is a principle that advocates for integrating security into the development and design of systems and applications from the outset. It prevents security vulnerabilities from being introduced later in the development process.

Compliance with laws, regulations, and industry standards is an integral part of information security. Organizations must adhere to legal and regulatory requirements relevant to their industry and geography.

Continuous monitoring and improvement is a principle that acknowledges the dynamic nature of information security. Security measures should be continually assessed and adjusted to address emerging threats and vulnerabilities.

Security is a shared responsibility that extends to all individuals and departments within an organization. It requires a collective effort to protect data and systems effectively.

In summary, understanding and applying these principles of information security is essential for safeguarding sensitive data, ensuring the integrity and availability of systems, and mitigating the ever-evolving threats in today's digital landscape.

In the realm of cybersecurity, understanding the various threats and attack vectors is crucial to building robust defenses. Threats come in many forms, ranging from cybercriminals seeking financial gain to state-sponsored hackers pursuing espionage or disruption. These threats can exploit a wide array of attack vectors, which are the avenues or methods used to compromise systems and networks.

One of the most common and persistent threats in the digital world is malware. Malware, short for malicious software, includes viruses, worms, Trojans, and other software designed to harm or gain unauthorized access to systems. Malware can infiltrate systems through infected files, email attachments, or compromised websites.

Phishing is another prevalent threat vector. Phishing attacks use deceptive emails or messages to trick recipients into revealing sensitive information, such as login credentials or financial details. These emails often appear legitimate, making it challenging for individuals to discern them from genuine communications.

Spear phishing is a targeted form of phishing where attackers tailor their messages to specific individuals or organizations, increasing the likelihood of success. Attackers gather information about their targets to craft convincing messages that exploit personal or professional interests.

Ransomware attacks have gained notoriety in recent years. Ransomware is a type of malware that encrypts a victim's files or systems, rendering them inaccessible. Attackers demand a ransom payment in exchange for the decryption key, making these attacks financially motivated. Ransomware can spread through phishing emails, malicious downloads, or vulnerable software.

Advanced Persistent Threats (APTs) are sophisticated and stealthy threats typically associated with state-sponsored actors or well-funded cybercriminal organizations. APTs involve prolonged and targeted attacks aimed at stealing sensitive data or maintaining persistent access to a target's network.

Zero-day vulnerabilities are a significant concern in the cybersecurity landscape. These are previously unknown software vulnerabilities that attackers can exploit before a patch or fix is available. Zero-day exploits are highly valuable and often traded on the black market.

Denial-of-Service (DoS) and Distributed Denial-of-Service (DDoS) attacks disrupt services or networks by overwhelming them with traffic. DoS attacks originate from a single source, while DDoS attacks involve a coordinated effort from multiple compromised devices or systems.

Social engineering attacks exploit human psychology to manipulate individuals into divulging information or taking specific actions. These attacks can occur in various forms, such as pretexting, baiting, or tailgating.

Physical security threats involve unauthorized access to physical premises or hardware. Attackers may attempt to gain entry to a secure facility, steal equipment, or compromise physical infrastructure.

Insider threats pose a unique challenge. These threats involve individuals within an organization who misuse their privileges or access to harm the organization, intentionally or unintentionally.

Supply chain attacks target vulnerabilities within a supply chain or third-party vendors to compromise the target organization. Attackers may infiltrate the supply chain to introduce malware or gain access to sensitive data.

IoT (Internet of Things) devices have introduced new attack vectors. Insecure IoT devices can be exploited to launch attacks or gain unauthorized access to networks. Weak default passwords and inadequate security practices are common vulnerabilities in IoT.

The Cloud presents both opportunities and security challenges. Cloud-based services and infrastructure are attractive targets for attackers. Misconfigured cloud resources, weak access controls, and unauthorized data exposure are common security issues.

Mobile devices are ubiquitous, making them prime targets for attackers. Mobile malware, malicious apps, and vulnerabilities in mobile operating systems can compromise the security and privacy of user data.

Web application vulnerabilities, such as SQL injection, Cross-Site Scripting (XSS), and Cross-Site Request Forgery (CSRF), expose web applications to exploitation. Attackers can compromise sensitive data or gain unauthorized access through these vulnerabilities.

Social media platforms are not immune to threats. Attackers use social media to distribute malware, launch phishing campaigns, or gather personal information about users.

The Internet of Things (IoT) encompasses a vast ecosystem of interconnected devices, from smart thermostats to industrial sensors. While IoT devices offer convenience and automation, they also introduce new security challenges.

Cyber-physical systems, such as industrial control systems (ICS) and critical infrastructure, are vulnerable to attacks that can have real-world consequences. Attacks on these systems can disrupt essential services, such as power grids or water treatment facilities.

Credential theft is a prevalent attack vector. Attackers steal login credentials through various means, including phishing, keyloggers, or exploiting weak passwords, to gain unauthorized access to systems and accounts.

Advanced evasion techniques are used by attackers to circumvent security measures and go undetected. These techniques involve obfuscating malicious code, exploiting vulnerabilities in security solutions, or manipulating network traffic.

While this overview highlights several threats and attack vectors, it's important to recognize that the threat landscape is constantly evolving. New threats and attack techniques emerge regularly, requiring organizations and individuals to remain vigilant, adapt their security measures, and stay informed about the latest developments in cybersecurity to mitigate risks effectively.

Chapter 3: Reconnaissance and Information Gathering

Exploring the world of cybersecurity, one quickly realizes that information gathering is a fundamental step in any successful cyberattack. Passive reconnaissance techniques play a crucial role in this initial phase, providing attackers with valuable insights without directly engaging with the target. Passive reconnaissance involves collecting information through methods that are unlikely to trigger alarms or raise suspicions.

One of the simplest and most widely used passive reconnaissance techniques is open-source intelligence (OSINT) gathering. OSINT involves mining publicly available information from various sources such as websites, social media, online forums, and public records. Attackers can gain insights into an organization's structure, personnel, technology stack, and potentially sensitive information by piecing together publicly accessible data.

Domain reconnaissance is a common practice that focuses on gathering information related to an organization's internet domain names. Tools and services like WHOIS databases, DNS (Domain Name System) records, and domain registrar information can provide valuable data, including domain ownership details, registration dates, and contact information.

Search engines play a significant role in passive reconnaissance. Attackers can use search engines to discover hidden information, such as sensitive documents, configuration files, or login pages inadvertently exposed on the web. Advanced search operators and techniques can narrow down search results to target specific information.

Passive DNS analysis involves studying historical DNS data to identify patterns and relationships between domain names, IP addresses, and infrastructure. This technique can help attackers map out an organization's network architecture and discover potentially vulnerable targets.

Network mapping and footprinting techniques aim to uncover an organization's digital footprint. This includes identifying IP address ranges, network topologies, and subdomains. Tools like Shodan, which scans the internet for open ports and services, can provide a comprehensive view of an organization's exposed assets.

Social media platforms are rich sources of information for passive reconnaissance. Attackers can gather data about employees, their roles, and even their interactions with colleagues. Employees' personal and professional connections on platforms like LinkedIn can help attackers identify potential targets for phishing attacks or social engineering.

Email addresses often reveal valuable information about an organization's naming conventions. Common email address patterns, such as "first.last@company.com" or "initials@company.com," can be used to guess the email addresses of employees. Attackers may also explore leaked or publicly available email lists.

Passive reconnaissance can extend to monitoring an organization's internet presence over time. By tracking changes in domain registrations, DNS records, or website content, attackers can detect shifts in an organization's strategy or technology stack. This information can be leveraged to tailor future attacks.

Threat intelligence feeds and databases provide a wealth of information on known threats, vulnerabilities, and attack indicators. Attackers can subscribe to or access these sources to gather insights into current cyber threats and weaknesses that may be exploitable.

While passive reconnaissance techniques can yield valuable information, it's essential to note that they operate within legal and ethical boundaries. Unauthorized access or data collection can lead to legal consequences. Responsible security professionals and ethical hackers use passive reconnaissance techniques as part of their legitimate efforts to identify and address vulnerabilities.

Organizations can defend against passive reconnaissance by implementing strong access controls, regularly monitoring their digital footprint, and educating employees about the risks of oversharing information online. Additionally, deploying intrusion detection systems and threat intelligence solutions can help organizations detect suspicious activities related to reconnaissance attempts.

In summary, passive reconnaissance techniques are an essential part of the information gathering phase in cybersecurity. They provide attackers with valuable insights while avoiding direct engagement with the target. Security professionals must remain vigilant and employ defensive measures to protect against passive reconnaissance attempts and mitigate potential risks.

As we delve deeper into the realm of cybersecurity, we encounter the concept of active reconnaissance methods, a crucial phase in the reconnaissance process. Unlike passive reconnaissance, where information is gathered passively without direct interaction, active reconnaissance involves actively probing a target's systems and networks to collect data. This phase provides attackers with more specific and detailed information but carries a higher risk of detection.

Port scanning is one of the fundamental active reconnaissance techniques. It involves sending network packets to target systems to identify open ports and services. By discovering open ports, attackers gain insights into the services running on a target's system, potentially identifying vulnerable services or applications.

Banner grabbing is a technique closely related to port scanning. It involves connecting to open ports and collecting banner information, which often reveals the type and version of the service or software running on that port. Banner grabbing helps attackers identify specific vulnerabilities associated with the service.

Network enumeration goes beyond port scanning to identify hosts, devices, and network resources within an organization's network. Attackers use various network enumeration tools and techniques to map out an organization's infrastructure, which can be valuable for planning further attacks.

Vulnerability scanning is a critical aspect of active reconnaissance. Vulnerability scanning tools assess target systems for known security vulnerabilities. Attackers use these tools to identify weaknesses that can be exploited to gain unauthorized access or compromise systems.

DNS enumeration involves querying Domain Name System (DNS) servers to discover information about a target's domain names and subdomains. Attackers can use DNS enumeration to uncover hidden or undocumented subdomains, potentially revealing overlooked entry points.

Service fingerprinting is a technique used to identify the specific software and versions running on target systems. Attackers use this information to tailor their attacks, selecting exploits that are likely to work against the detected services.

Operating system fingerprinting aims to determine the operating system running on a target host. Attackers can use this information to choose attacks and payloads that are compatible with the target's operating system.

Ping sweeps involve sending ICMP (Internet Control Message Protocol) echo requests to a range of IP addresses to identify live hosts on a network. This technique helps attackers identify active targets within a larger network.

Traceroute is a network diagnostic tool that reveals the path packets take to reach a target host. Attackers use traceroute to map out the network topology, identifying routers, firewalls, and other network devices.

Exploitation of known vulnerabilities is a riskier form of active reconnaissance. Once vulnerabilities are identified, attackers may attempt to exploit them to gain unauthorized access or control over target systems.

Brute force attacks involve systematically trying all possible combinations of usernames and passwords to gain access to a system or application. Attackers use brute force techniques to crack weak or default credentials.

Credential stuffing is a form of attack where attackers use previously stolen username and password combinations to gain unauthorized access to other accounts. This method relies on individuals reusing passwords across multiple services.

Active reconnaissance techniques require careful planning and execution, as they can trigger security alerts and intrusion detection systems. Ethical hackers and security professionals use these methods to identify and remediate vulnerabilities in their own systems, ensuring that they are adequately protected against potential threats.

To defend against active reconnaissance, organizations implement intrusion detection and prevention systems, monitor network traffic for suspicious activities, and regularly update and patch their systems to address known vulnerabilities. Security awareness training for employees also plays a critical role in preventing successful attacks initiated through social engineering and other active reconnaissance methods.

In summary, active reconnaissance methods represent a proactive approach to gathering information about target systems and networks. While they provide attackers with more specific and detailed data, they come with a higher risk of detection. Security professionals employ these techniques to assess and enhance their own systems' security, while organizations implement defensive measures to protect against potential threats.

Chapter 4: Vulnerability Assessment and Scanning

In the ever-evolving landscape of cybersecurity, one of the critical tasks is identifying vulnerabilities in systems. Vulnerabilities are weaknesses or flaws in software, hardware, configurations, or processes that can be exploited by malicious actors. Identifying these vulnerabilities is a fundamental step in securing digital assets and preventing potential breaches.

Vulnerability assessment is a systematic process used to identify and prioritize vulnerabilities in a system or network. It involves the use of various tools, techniques, and methodologies to scan and analyze the target environment for weaknesses. One primary goal of vulnerability assessment is to provide organizations with actionable insights into their security posture.

Automated vulnerability scanning tools are commonly used in the initial stages of vulnerability assessment. These tools scan systems and networks to identify known vulnerabilities by comparing their configurations and software versions against a database of known issues and patches. Vulnerability scanners provide a starting point for further investigation.

Manual testing is an essential aspect of vulnerability assessment. While automated tools can detect known vulnerabilities, they may not identify novel or unique weaknesses. Skilled security professionals conduct manual testing to explore potential vulnerabilities that automated scanners may overlook. This hands-on approach often involves trying to exploit vulnerabilities to validate their existence and assess their impact.

Penetration testing, or pen testing, is a more comprehensive form of vulnerability assessment. It simulates real-world attacks by attempting to exploit identified vulnerabilities in a controlled and ethical manner. Penetration testers, often referred to as ethical hackers, use their expertise to assess the security of systems, applications, and networks.

Web application assessments focus on identifying vulnerabilities specific to web applications, such as SQL injection, Cross-Site Scripting (XSS), and Cross-Site Request Forgery (CSRF). These assessments involve scrutinizing web applications for security flaws that could lead to unauthorized access, data breaches, or other forms of exploitation.

Network vulnerability assessments aim to uncover weaknesses in the network infrastructure, including routers, firewalls, switches, and other devices. These assessments help organizations understand potential entry points and points of failure within their network.

Wireless network assessments focus on evaluating the security of wireless networks and devices. Attackers can exploit weaknesses in wireless networks to gain unauthorized access or intercept sensitive information. Assessments identify vulnerabilities in wireless encryption, configuration, and access controls. Cloud security assessments are tailored to evaluate the security of cloud-based infrastructure and services. Organizations increasingly rely on cloud providers for hosting and storing data, making it crucial to assess the security of these environments for potential misconfigurations and vulnerabilities.

Database assessments scrutinize database systems for vulnerabilities that could expose sensitive data. Security professionals assess database configurations, user access controls, and the security of data stored within the database.

Social engineering assessments involve testing an organization's susceptibility to manipulation and deception by simulating phishing attacks, impersonation attempts, and other social engineering tactics. These assessments assess the effectiveness of security awareness programs and employee training.

External and internal assessments distinguish between vulnerabilities that are accessible from outside an organization's network (external) and those that may be exploited from within (internal). Internal assessments are valuable for identifying risks associated with insider threats.

Continuous monitoring is a proactive approach to identifying vulnerabilities. It involves continuously monitoring systems, networks, and applications for changes, anomalies, and potential security weaknesses. Continuous monitoring allows organizations to detect vulnerabilities as they emerge or evolve over time.

Bug bounty programs offer organizations a unique approach to identifying vulnerabilities. These programs incentivize independent security researchers, often called "bug hunters," to discover and report vulnerabilities in exchange for rewards or recognition. Bug bounty programs harness the power of a global community of security experts to uncover vulnerabilities.

Patch management is a critical component of vulnerability management. Once vulnerabilities are identified, organizations must prioritize and apply patches or security updates to mitigate the associated risks. Timely patching reduces the window of opportunity for attackers to exploit vulnerabilities.

In summary, identifying vulnerabilities in systems is an ongoing and multifaceted process in the world of cybersecurity. It involves a combination of automated scanning, manual testing, ethical hacking, and continuous monitoring. By systematically identifying and addressing vulnerabilities, organizations can enhance their security posture and reduce the risk of cyberattacks and data breaches.

In the field of cybersecurity, scanning and enumeration tools play a pivotal role in identifying vulnerabilities and mapping the digital terrain of target systems and networks. These tools are essential components of the reconnaissance phase, allowing security professionals and ethical hackers to gather critical information about the assets they intend to protect or assess. Port scanning tools are among the most commonly used scanning and enumeration tools. They enable users to probe a target's systems for open ports and services. By identifying open ports, security professionals can determine which services are running on a target system, potentially exposing vulnerabilities.

Nmap, short for Network Mapper, is a widely recognized and versatile open-source port scanning tool. It provides a comprehensive range of scanning techniques, including TCP, UDP, and SYN scans, and can detect the operating system and versions of services running on target systems.

Banner grabbing tools complement port scanning by collecting banner information from open ports. This information often reveals details about the type and version of the service or software running on a specific port, aiding in vulnerability assessment and exploitation.

Wireshark is a popular network protocol analyzer that allows users to capture and examine network traffic. While not a scanning tool in the traditional sense, Wireshark is invaluable for analyzing the data exchanged between systems, identifying potential vulnerabilities, and understanding network behavior.

Network mapping tools are essential for enumerating a target's network infrastructure. These tools create a visual map of the network, including routers, switches, firewalls, and connected devices, helping security professionals understand the network's topology.

One well-known network mapping tool is Netstat, which provides information about active network connections and listening ports on a system. It allows users to identify established connections and potentially rogue or unauthorized network activity.

Automated vulnerability scanners are essential enumeration tools that assess target systems for known vulnerabilities. These scanners leverage databases of known vulnerabilities and their associated patches to identify weaknesses in software, configurations, or systems.

OpenVAS (Open Vulnerability Assessment System) is a robust open-source vulnerability scanner that assists security professionals in identifying and prioritizing vulnerabilities. It performs comprehensive scans and provides detailed reports on discovered vulnerabilities.

DNS enumeration tools are specifically designed to query DNS servers and extract information about domain names and subdomains associated with a target organization. DNS information can reveal hidden or undocumented network assets.

TheHarvester is a versatile DNS enumeration tool that collects information from various public sources, including search engines, public databases, and DNS servers. It assists in building a comprehensive list of subdomains and email addresses associated with a target domain.

SNMP enumeration tools focus on discovering devices and gathering information from SNMP (Simple Network Management Protocol)-enabled devices on a network. SNMP is commonly used to monitor and manage network devices.

Enumerating the SNMP community strings used for authentication is an important aspect of SNMP enumeration. Tools like SNMPwalk and SNMPget allow users to query SNMP agents and retrieve information about devices, including their configurations and performance metrics.

SMTP enumeration tools concentrate on probing email servers for information about users and email addresses. They can help attackers identify potential targets for phishing attacks or email-based social engineering.

SMTP user enumeration is a specific type of SMTP enumeration that focuses on verifying the existence of valid email addresses on an email server. Tools like SMTP-user-enum automate the process of checking which email addresses are active on a target server.

SNMP enumeration tools concentrate on probing email servers for information about users and email addresses.

They can help attackers identify potential targets for phishing attacks or email-based social engineering.

SMB enumeration tools are used to enumerate resources, shares, and users on Windows-based networks that use the Server Message Block (SMB) protocol. These tools help identify weaknesses in network configurations and permissions.

SMBclient is a command-line utility that allows users to connect to and interact with SMB shares on remote Windows systems. It can be used to enumerate shared resources and retrieve information about user accounts.

LDAP enumeration tools focus on querying LDAP (Lightweight Directory Access Protocol) servers to gather information about directory services, users, groups, and permissions. LDAP is commonly used in authentication and directory services.

Ldapsearch is a command-line tool that enables users to search LDAP directories and retrieve information about users, groups, and attributes. It is invaluable for enumerating directory services and user accounts.

In summary, scanning and enumeration tools are indispensable in the field of cybersecurity for identifying vulnerabilities and mapping the digital landscape of target systems and networks. These tools empower security professionals and ethical hackers to gather essential information about the assets they aim to secure or assess, ultimately enhancing the security posture of organizations and systems.

Chapter 5: Exploiting Common System Weaknesses

In the ever-evolving landscape of cybersecurity, understanding common vulnerabilities and exploits is paramount for safeguarding digital assets and systems. Vulnerabilities are weaknesses or flaws in software, hardware, configurations, or processes that can be exploited by malicious actors. Exploits are techniques or tools used to take advantage of these vulnerabilities to compromise systems or gain unauthorized access.

One of the most prevalent vulnerabilities in the digital world is unpatched software. Failing to apply security patches and updates leaves systems exposed to known vulnerabilities that attackers can exploit. Keeping software up-to-date is a crucial defense against this common vulnerability.

SQL injection is a widespread and critical vulnerability in web applications. Attackers exploit this vulnerability by injecting malicious SQL code into input fields, which can lead to unauthorized access to databases, data theft, or data manipulation. Proper input validation and parameterized queries are effective defenses against SQL injection.

Cross-Site Scripting (XSS) is another prevalent web application vulnerability. It occurs when untrusted data is displayed on a web page without proper sanitization, allowing attackers to inject malicious scripts that can steal user data or perform actions on behalf of the user.

Implementing output encoding and input validation can mitigate XSS vulnerabilities.

Cross-Site Request Forgery (CSRF) is a vulnerability that tricks users into performing actions on a website without their consent. Attackers can exploit CSRF vulnerabilities to perform actions on behalf of authenticated users, potentially leading to unauthorized changes or data loss. Implementing anti-CSRF tokens is an effective countermeasure.

Insecure authentication mechanisms are common vulnerabilities that can lead to unauthorized access. Weak or default passwords, inadequate password policies, and poor session management can all contribute to insecure authentication. Organizations should enforce strong password policies and implement multi-factor authentication (MFA) to mitigate these vulnerabilities.

Buffer overflows are vulnerabilities that occur when an application writes data beyond the allocated buffer space. Attackers can exploit buffer overflows to execute malicious code, potentially compromising the system. Proper input validation and secure coding practices can prevent buffer overflows.

Insecure deserialization is a vulnerability that occurs when data is deserialized without proper validation. Attackers can manipulate serialized data to execute arbitrary code or perform malicious actions. Implementing input validation and using trusted serialization libraries can mitigate this vulnerability.

Security misconfigurations are common weaknesses that arise from improperly configured software, servers, or applications. Attackers can exploit these misconfigurations to gain unauthorized access or expose sensitive data. Regular security assessments and audits can help identify and remediate misconfigurations.

Sensitive data exposure occurs when organizations fail to adequately protect sensitive information, such as credit card numbers or personal data. Attackers can exploit this vulnerability to steal sensitive data for financial gain or identity theft. Encrypting data at rest and in transit, as well as implementing strong access controls, can protect against data exposure.

XML External Entity (XXE) attacks target applications that process XML input without proper validation. Attackers can use XXE to read sensitive files or execute arbitrary code on the server. Disabling external entity expansion and input validation can prevent XXE vulnerabilities.

Remote code execution vulnerabilities allow attackers to execute code on a target system remotely. These vulnerabilities often result from insecure input handling or insufficient access controls. Regularly patching software and conducting code reviews can help mitigate remote code execution vulnerabilities.

Insecure APIs (Application Programming Interfaces) are vulnerabilities in the interfaces used for communication between software components. Attackers can exploit insecure APIs to access sensitive data or perform unauthorized actions. Securing APIs with proper authentication and access controls is essential.

Unvalidated redirects and forwards occur when web applications redirect users to external websites or resources without proper validation. Attackers can abuse this vulnerability to trick users into visiting malicious sites. Validating redirects and using whitelists for allowed destinations can prevent this type of exploit.

Zero-day vulnerabilities are vulnerabilities that are not yet known to the software vendor or the public. Attackers can exploit zero-day vulnerabilities before patches or fixes are available. Staying informed about emerging threats and vulnerabilities is crucial for proactive defense.

The OWASP Top Ten is a widely recognized list of common vulnerabilities and exploits in web applications. It serves as a valuable resource for organizations seeking to prioritize their security efforts and address these prevalent issues.

In summary, understanding common vulnerabilities and exploits is essential for protecting digital assets and systems from cyber threats. By identifying and addressing these vulnerabilities through best practices, secure coding, and regular updates, organizations can enhance their security posture and reduce the risk of exploitation. In the world of cybersecurity, the notion of gaining unauthorized access is a topic of critical importance. Unauthorized access refers to the act of accessing a system, network, application, or data without proper authorization or consent. It is a fundamental security concern and a primary objective for malicious actors seeking to compromise digital assets.

Unauthorized access can take various forms, and understanding these methods is essential for defending against potential breaches. One of the most straightforward methods is through weak or compromised passwords. Attackers often attempt to guess passwords or use stolen credentials to gain entry. Therefore, strong password policies and multi-factor authentication are crucial defenses.

Brute force attacks represent a persistent and straightforward approach to gaining unauthorized access. In these attacks, attackers systematically try all possible combinations of usernames and passwords until they discover the correct combination. This method relies on the assumption that some users may choose weak or easily guessable passwords.

Dictionary attacks are similar to brute force attacks but involve trying common words, phrases, or passwords found in dictionaries. Attackers compile lists of commonly used passwords and use them in their attempts to gain unauthorized access. Organizations can defend against these attacks by enforcing password complexity requirements and regularly updating password lists.

Credential stuffing is a tactic where attackers use previously stolen username and password combinations to gain unauthorized access to other accounts. This method takes advantage of individuals who reuse passwords across multiple services. To protect against credential stuffing, individuals should use unique passwords for different accounts.

Phishing attacks are a prevalent method for tricking users into revealing their login credentials or other sensitive information. Attackers use deceptive emails, messages, or websites that mimic legitimate ones to persuade individuals to enter their credentials. Security awareness training and email filtering are essential defenses against phishing.

Keyloggers are malicious software or hardware devices that record keystrokes on a victim's computer, capturing login credentials and other sensitive information. Regularly updating and using reputable antivirus software can help detect and remove keyloggers.

Man-in-the-middle (MitM) attacks occur when an attacker intercepts communications between two parties, such as a user and a server. In these attacks, the attacker can capture login credentials or manipulate data. Employing secure communication protocols like HTTPS and using trusted networks can mitigate MitM attacks.

Session hijacking or session fixation attacks involve attackers taking control of an active user session on a web application. Attackers may steal session cookies or tokens to impersonate a user and gain unauthorized access. Implementing secure session management practices can help prevent session hijacking.

Inadequate access controls can lead to unauthorized access within an organization's own systems. Insufficient access control settings, misconfigured permissions, or failure to revoke access when it is no longer needed can all contribute to this vulnerability. Regularly reviewing and updating access controls is essential.

Privilege escalation attacks involve attackers gaining higher levels of access or privileges within a system or application. By exploiting vulnerabilities or weaknesses, attackers can elevate their privileges and potentially gain control over critical systems. Employing the principle of least privilege and implementing proper access controls can mitigate this risk.

Backdoors are hidden or unauthorized methods of access that are intentionally or unintentionally left in systems or applications. Attackers can exploit backdoors to gain access even if other security measures are in place. Regularly auditing and scanning for backdoors is essential for defense.

Zero-day vulnerabilities are vulnerabilities that are not yet known to the software vendor or the public. Attackers may discover and exploit these vulnerabilities before patches or fixes are available. Staying informed about emerging threats and applying patches promptly is crucial for defense.

Social engineering tactics involve manipulating individuals into divulging sensitive information or performing actions that aid in unauthorized access. Attackers may use pretexting, baiting, or tailgating to deceive individuals. Security awareness training and education can help individuals recognize and resist social engineering attempts.

Physical security breaches occur when attackers gain physical access to an organization's premises or hardware. They may steal devices, gain access to servers or data centers, or compromise physical infrastructure. Robust physical security measures, such as access controls and surveillance, are vital defenses.

Exploiting software vulnerabilities is a common method for gaining unauthorized access. Attackers search for and exploit weaknesses in software or applications to compromise systems. Regularly updating and patching software is essential for defense.

In summary, gaining unauthorized access is a persistent and multifaceted threat in the realm of cybersecurity. Understanding the various methods and vulnerabilities that attackers exploit is crucial for organizations and individuals seeking to protect their digital assets. By implementing strong security practices, conducting regular audits, and staying informed about emerging threats, it is possible to mitigate the risks associated with unauthorized access.

Chapter 6: Password Cracking and Authentication Attacks

In the realm of cybersecurity, one encounters the concept of brute force attacks, a method employed by malicious actors to gain unauthorized access to systems, applications, or data. These attacks represent a straightforward and relentless approach, where attackers systematically attempt all possible combinations of usernames and passwords until they discover the correct credentials.

Brute force attacks exploit the vulnerability of weak or easily guessable passwords, emphasizing the importance of robust password policies and the adoption of multi-factor authentication (MFA) as essential defenses against such intrusions. It's worth noting that even seemingly strong passwords can be vulnerable to brute force attacks if they lack complexity or if users fall into predictable patterns when creating them.

The fundamental premise of a brute force attack is to exhaustively try every possible password combination within a given character set, making it a time-consuming process. Attackers use specialized software or scripts to automate this process, allowing them to test thousands or even millions of combinations per second.

One common scenario where brute force attacks are employed is in gaining unauthorized access to user accounts. Attackers target login pages or authentication mechanisms, repeatedly trying different username and password combinations until they find the correct ones. This method is effective if users have weak or easily guessable passwords.

To mitigate the risk of brute force attacks, organizations should enforce password complexity requirements. This includes mandating the use of a combination of uppercase and lowercase letters, numbers, and special characters. Passwords should also be of sufficient length to resist brute force attempts.

Multi-factor authentication (MFA) is a robust defense against brute force attacks. MFA requires users to provide multiple forms of verification, such as a password and a one-time code sent to their mobile device, before gaining access. Even if an attacker guesses the correct password, they would still need the additional factor to log in.

Dictionary attacks are a variation of brute force attacks where attackers use common words, phrases, or passwords found in dictionaries. These attacks rely on the fact that some users choose easily guessable passwords or use common words as their passwords. Implementing password policies that prevent the use of dictionary words can help mitigate dictionary attacks.

Attackers often compile lists of commonly used passwords and known password patterns to streamline their brute force or dictionary attack efforts. Organizations can defend against these precompiled attack lists by regularly updating and modifying their password policies and avoiding commonly used patterns.

Rate limiting and account lockout mechanisms are effective countermeasures against brute force attacks. Rate limiting restricts the number of login attempts a user can make within a specified time frame. Account lockout policies temporarily lock user accounts after a certain number of failed login attempts, preventing further attempts by attackers.

Additionally, organizations can implement intrusion detection systems (IDS) and intrusion prevention systems (IPS) to detect and block suspicious login attempts. These systems can recognize patterns indicative of brute force attacks and take actions to protect the targeted accounts or systems.

While brute force attacks are relatively straightforward, they can be time-consuming and resource-intensive. Attackers must have the patience to persistently test a vast number of combinations. Consequently, implementing strong password policies, MFA, and other security measures significantly raises the bar for potential attackers.

In some cases, attackers may resort to hybrid attacks, combining brute force methods with other techniques to increase their chances of success. For example, attackers may use a dictionary attack to try commonly used passwords before resorting to a full brute force attempt. Organizations should remain vigilant and employ multiple layers of defense to mitigate such hybrid attacks.

In summary, brute force attacks represent a persistent and resource-intensive method employed by malicious actors to gain unauthorized access to systems, applications, or data. Organizations and individuals can defend against these attacks by implementing robust password policies, adopting multi-factor authentication, and using additional security measures such as rate limiting, account lockout, and intrusion detection systems. By understanding the nature of brute force attacks and implementing best practices, one can significantly reduce the risk of falling victim to these intrusions.

In the realm of cybersecurity, password cracking tools and techniques occupy a significant place in the arsenal of both attackers and defenders. Passwords are a ubiquitous form of authentication, and their security is paramount in safeguarding digital assets. However, the effectiveness of passwords hinges on their complexity and the measures in place to protect them.

Password cracking refers to the process of attempting to recover or guess passwords through various methods, and it is a critical aspect of penetration testing and security assessments. Security professionals use password cracking techniques to assess the strength of passwords and identify vulnerabilities in authentication systems.

One common approach in password cracking is the use of dictionary attacks. In this technique, attackers utilize a list of commonly used words, phrases, or passwords, known as a dictionary, to systematically guess passwords. Attackers may augment the dictionary with variations, such as appending numbers or symbols, to increase their chances of success.

Brute force attacks represent a more exhaustive method of password cracking. Attackers employ software or scripts that systematically try every possible combination of characters within a given character set until they discover the correct password. Brute force attacks are resource-intensive and time-consuming but can be effective against weak passwords.

Rainbow tables are precomputed tables of password hashes that significantly expedite the password cracking process. Attackers can compare stolen password hashes to entries in a rainbow table to quickly identify corresponding passwords. Employing salting, which adds random data to passwords before hashing, can mitigate the effectiveness of rainbow table attacks.

Password spraying is a technique where attackers attempt a limited number of passwords against multiple user accounts. Unlike traditional brute force attacks, password spraying is less likely to trigger account lockouts or alarms, making it a stealthier method for attackers.

Credential stuffing is an attack method where attackers use previously stolen username and password combinations to gain unauthorized access to other accounts. This tactic relies on individuals reusing passwords across multiple services, highlighting the importance of using unique passwords for different accounts.

Hybrid attacks combine elements of both dictionary and brute force attacks. Attackers use dictionaries to try common words and phrases before resorting to brute force methods. This approach is more efficient than pure brute force but more thorough than dictionary attacks alone.

Password cracking tools have evolved to become sophisticated and efficient, enabling attackers to crack passwords more effectively. Tools like John the Ripper and Hashcat are well-known for their capabilities in password cracking. These tools support various algorithms and attack modes, making them versatile for different scenarios.

To defend against password cracking attacks, organizations should implement strong password policies that mandate complex passwords with a combination of uppercase and lowercase letters, numbers, and special characters. Passwords should also have a minimum length requirement to resist brute force attacks.

Multi-factor authentication (MFA) is a powerful defense against password cracking. MFA requires users to provide multiple forms of verification, such as a password and a one-time code sent to their mobile device, before gaining access. Even if attackers crack a password, they would still need the additional factor to log in.

Rate limiting and account lockout mechanisms can mitigate password spraying and brute force attacks. Rate limiting restricts the number of login attempts a user can make within a specified time frame. Account lockout policies temporarily lock user accounts after a certain number of failed login attempts, preventing further attempts by attackers.

Additionally, the use of strong encryption algorithms to protect stored passwords is essential. Hashing and salting passwords before storage makes it significantly more challenging for attackers to recover plaintext passwords, even if they compromise the hashed values.

Regularly updating and patching systems and applications is crucial to prevent attackers from exploiting known vulnerabilities to gain unauthorized access. Vulnerability management helps organizations stay ahead of potential threats.

Password cracking is not limited to malicious purposes. Ethical hackers and security professionals use password cracking techniques as part of penetration testing and security assessments to identify weaknesses in authentication systems and help organizations improve their security posture.

In summary, password cracking tools and techniques are a double-edged sword in the world of cybersecurity. While they pose a threat to the security of digital assets, they also serve as valuable tools for security professionals to assess and enhance the strength of authentication systems. Employing strong password policies, multi-factor authentication, rate limiting, and account lockout mechanisms are crucial measures to defend against password cracking attacks and protect sensitive information.

Chapter 7: Social Engineering Techniques

In the vast landscape of cybersecurity, the topics of phishing and spear phishing stand as critical concerns, representing deceptive techniques employed by malicious actors to manipulate individuals and organizations. Phishing, in its broader sense, encompasses fraudulent attempts to trick individuals into divulging sensitive information, such as login credentials, credit card numbers, or personal data.

The fundamental concept of phishing involves the use of deceptive tactics to create a false sense of trust or urgency, enticing victims to take actions that benefit the attackers. These actions may include clicking on malicious links, downloading infected files, or providing sensitive information to what appears to be a legitimate source.

Email phishing is one of the most common and widely recognized forms of phishing. Attackers send deceptive emails that mimic trustworthy sources, such as banks, social media platforms, or government agencies. These emails often contain urgent requests, alarming messages, or offers that prompt recipients to click on links or download attachments.

Spear phishing is a more targeted and sophisticated variant of phishing. In spear phishing attacks, attackers customize their deceptive messages to target specific individuals, often using information obtained through reconnaissance. This personalization makes spear phishing particularly effective, as victims are more likely to trust messages that appear tailored to their interests or circumstances.

A key element of successful phishing and spear phishing attacks is the creation of fraudulent websites or login pages that closely mimic legitimate ones. These imitation sites aim to deceive victims into entering their credentials, ultimately allowing attackers to harvest sensitive information.

Phishing attacks can also take the form of text messages, known as smishing, or voice messages, known as vishing. Smishing involves sending deceptive text messages that prompt recipients to click on links or provide personal information, while vishing uses voice messages or phone calls to deceive victims into divulging sensitive information.

One prevalent tactic in phishing is the use of URL manipulation. Attackers create links that appear to lead to legitimate websites but actually direct victims to malicious sites. Hovering over links to inspect the URL before clicking is a simple but effective defense against this tactic.

Another deception method involves the use of malicious attachments. Attackers send emails with seemingly harmless file attachments, which, when opened, execute malicious code on the victim's device. Employing robust email filtering and antivirus software is crucial for detecting and blocking malicious attachments.

Phishing emails often contain urgent or alarming language to pressure recipients into taking immediate action. These tactics are designed to create a sense of panic or fear, causing individuals to overlook red flags. Training and educating individuals to recognize and remain calm in the face of such messages is essential.

Spear phishing relies on personalized information to gain the trust of victims. Attackers may reference the recipient's name, job title, or recent activities to create a convincing facade. It is vital for individuals and organizations to be cautious when sharing personal or professional information online.

Phishing and spear phishing are not limited to email; attackers leverage social engineering tactics in these attacks. By manipulating human psychology, attackers exploit trust, curiosity, or fear to trick victims into taking actions that benefit the attacker.

One common tactic is pretexting, where attackers create elaborate backstories or scenarios to deceive individuals. For example, an attacker might impersonate a colleague in an email, claiming to need urgent assistance or requesting sensitive information.

Phishing and spear phishing often target employees within organizations. Attackers understand that employees may have access to valuable corporate data or financial information. Organizations must implement robust security training programs to educate employees about the risks and tactics associated with phishing attacks.

Multi-factor authentication (MFA) is a powerful defense against phishing attacks. MFA requires users to provide multiple forms of verification, such as a password and a one-time code sent to their mobile device, before gaining access. Even if attackers obtain login credentials, they would still need the additional factor to access accounts.

Regularly updating and patching software is crucial to prevent attackers from exploiting known vulnerabilities to deliver phishing payloads. Vulnerability management helps organizations stay ahead of potential threats.

In summary, phishing and spear phishing represent insidious threats in the cybersecurity landscape, exploiting human psychology and trust to deceive individuals and organizations. Recognizing the tactics and red flags associated with these attacks, implementing robust email filtering and antivirus solutions, and educating individuals about the risks are essential steps in defending against phishing and spear phishing attempts. Additionally, multi-factor authentication and a culture of cybersecurity awareness contribute significantly to strengthening defenses against these deceptive tactics.

In the intricate realm of cybersecurity, the subjects of pretexting and baiting emerge as deceptive tactics employed by malicious actors to manipulate individuals and organizations. These tactics fall under the umbrella of social engineering, which involves exploiting human psychology and trust to deceive victims.

Pretexting is a method of deception where attackers create elaborate backstories or scenarios to trick individuals into divulging sensitive information or taking specific actions. The goal is to gain the victim's trust by posing as someone credible or legitimate. For example, an attacker might impersonate a bank employee, claiming to need account information for verification purposes.

To make pretexting more convincing, attackers often conduct extensive research to gather information about the target. This information may include the target's name, job title, workplace, and even recent activities. Armed with this personalized data, attackers can craft a convincing narrative that resonates with the victim.

One common pretexting scenario involves a phone call or email from someone claiming to be an IT technician or support agent. The attacker might state that they've detected a security issue with the victim's computer and need remote access to resolve the problem. Unsuspecting victims may grant access, unwittingly exposing their systems to exploitation.

Another pretexting tactic is the impersonation of a colleague or supervisor within an organization. Attackers may send emails or messages requesting sensitive information or urgent actions. Employees, believing they are communicating with a trusted colleague, may unknowingly comply with the attacker's requests.

Baiting is another form of social engineering that leverages the lure of something enticing to deceive victims. Attackers offer victims a seemingly valuable reward, such as a free download, discount coupon, or intriguing file. However, these offers come with a hidden catch: the bait is malicious, designed to compromise the victim's system.

For example, attackers might create a fake website offering free software downloads that appear legitimate. Once a victim downloads and runs the software, malware is installed on their system. This malware can steal sensitive data, monitor activities, or provide attackers with remote access.

USB baiting is a physical form of baiting where attackers leave infected USB drives in public places or workplaces. Curious individuals who discover the drives may plug them into their computers, unknowingly introducing malware to their systems. This tactic relies on human curiosity and the temptation to explore unknown content.

Social engineering tactics like pretexting and baiting exploit common human traits, including trust, curiosity, and the desire for rewards. Attackers are skilled at creating persuasive scenarios and using psychological manipulation to deceive victims.

Organizations must prioritize security awareness training to educate employees about these deceptive tactics. Employees should be cautious when sharing sensitive information, especially with individuals they have not verified. Verifying the identity of requestors through separate channels, such as a phone call to a known number, can help prevent falling victim to pretexting.

To defend against baiting, individuals should exercise caution when encountering enticing offers or unknown USB drives. It's essential to maintain a healthy level of skepticism and verify the legitimacy of offers or files before taking any action. Employing robust antivirus and anti-malware solutions can also help detect and mitigate threats.

Multi-factor authentication (MFA) is a valuable defense against pretexting attempts. MFA requires users to provide multiple forms of verification, such as a password and a one-time code sent to their mobile device, before gaining access. Even if attackers obtain login credentials through pretexting, they would still need the additional factor to access accounts.

In summary, pretexting and baiting represent deceptive tactics within the broader scope of social engineering, exploiting human psychology and trust to manipulate victims. Awareness, skepticism, and verification are key defenses against these tactics. By educating individuals about the risks and implementing security measures like multi-factor authentication and robust antivirus solutions, organizations and individuals can strengthen their defenses against pretexting and baiting attempts.

Chapter 8: Malware and Payload Delivery

In the complex realm of cybersecurity, the term "malware" stands as a pivotal concept, encompassing a wide array of malicious software designed to infiltrate, disrupt, or compromise computer systems, networks, and data. Understanding the various types of malware is fundamental in fortifying defenses against these insidious threats.

One of the most common types of malware is the computer virus. Viruses are self-replicating programs that attach themselves to legitimate files or applications, infecting them in the process. When infected files are executed, the virus spreads and can corrupt or damage data, leading to system instability or data loss.

Worms are another type of malware that, unlike viruses, do not require a host file to propagate. Worms are standalone programs that can spread rapidly across networks, exploiting vulnerabilities and infecting multiple systems. Their ability to self-replicate and propagate makes them particularly dangerous.

Trojan horses, often referred to as Trojans, are deceptive malware that masquerade as legitimate software or files. Once a Trojan is executed, it performs malicious actions without the user's knowledge. Trojans can steal sensitive information, create backdoors for attackers, or damage systems.

Spyware is a category of malware designed to spy on users' activities without their consent. Spyware can monitor keystrokes, capture screenshots, record browsing habits, and gather sensitive data. This information is often sent to remote servers for malicious purposes.

Adware, although less malicious than other types of malware, can be highly annoying. Adware displays intrusive advertisements, pop-ups, or banners to generate revenue for the attacker. While not inherently harmful, adware can disrupt user experiences and compromise system performance.

Ransomware has gained notoriety in recent years as a particularly destructive form of malware. Ransomware encrypts a victim's files or entire system, rendering them inaccessible. Attackers then demand a ransom from the victim in exchange for the decryption key. Paying the ransom is discouraged, as it does not guarantee the return of data and may further fund criminal activities.

Rootkits are stealthy malware designed to provide attackers with unauthorized access to a compromised system. Rootkits often hide their presence and activities from traditional security software, making them challenging to detect. They can grant attackers full control over a system.

Botnets are networks of compromised computers or devices, often controlled remotely by a single entity. Each compromised device in a botnet, known as a bot, can be instructed to perform various malicious activities, such as sending spam emails, launching distributed denial-of-service (DDoS) attacks, or stealing data.

Keyloggers are a type of spyware that records every keystroke made by a user, capturing sensitive information such as usernames, passwords, and credit card numbers. Attackers can use this data for identity theft or other malicious purposes.

Fileless malware is a relatively new and stealthy category of malware that operates in the computer's memory without leaving traditional traces on the hard drive. This makes it difficult to detect using traditional antivirus software. Fileless malware often leverages legitimate system tools and processes for its malicious activities.

Mobile malware is designed to target mobile devices, such as smartphones and tablets. Mobile malware can take various forms, including Trojans, spyware, and adware, and can compromise the security and privacy of mobile users.

Macro viruses are a type of malware that exploits macros, which are scripts or code segments embedded in documents and spreadsheets. When a user opens an infected document, the macro virus is executed, allowing it to spread or perform malicious actions.

Bootkits are a type of rootkit that infects the system's master boot record (MBR) or boot sector. Bootkits gain control of the system during the boot process, allowing attackers to maintain persistence and control over the compromised system.

Polymorphic malware is designed to constantly change its code or appearance to evade detection by antivirus software. Each iteration of the malware appears different, making it challenging for security tools to recognize and block.

Metamorphic malware is a more advanced form of polymorphic malware that not only changes its appearance but also its underlying code structure with each iteration. This level of complexity makes metamorphic malware even more elusive to traditional security measures.

Understanding the diverse landscape of malware is crucial in developing effective strategies to combat these threats. Security professionals and organizations must employ a combination of robust antivirus software, intrusion detection systems, regular system updates, and user education to mitigate the risks posed by malware. Staying informed about emerging malware trends and evolving defense strategies is essential in the ongoing battle against these malicious entities.

In the intricate realm of cybersecurity, the topic of exploiting software vulnerabilities is a critical concern, representing a method employed by malicious actors to compromise computer systems, applications, and networks. Understanding the mechanisms behind software vulnerabilities and how attackers exploit them is essential in fortifying defenses against these threats.

Software vulnerabilities, also known as security vulnerabilities or security flaws, are weaknesses or flaws in computer software that can be exploited by attackers to gain unauthorized access, disrupt operations, or compromise data. These vulnerabilities can exist in operating systems, web applications, mobile apps, or any software component that interacts with a computer system.

One common type of software vulnerability is known as a buffer overflow. In a buffer overflow vulnerability, an attacker sends more data to a software buffer than it can handle, causing the excess data to overwrite adjacent memory areas. By carefully crafting the input data, attackers can manipulate the program's behavior and potentially execute malicious code.

Another prevalent vulnerability is the injection attack, which includes SQL injection and cross-site scripting (XSS). SQL injection occurs when an attacker inserts malicious SQL statements into input fields, manipulating database queries to extract or modify data. XSS, on the other hand, involves injecting malicious scripts into web pages viewed by other users, potentially leading to data theft or session hijacking.

Authentication and session management vulnerabilities can allow attackers to impersonate users or gain unauthorized access. These vulnerabilities may include weak password policies, predictable session identifiers, or improper authentication mechanisms. Attackers exploit these weaknesses to assume control over user accounts.

Zero-day vulnerabilities are particularly concerning because they are unknown to the software vendor and have not yet been patched. Attackers discover and exploit these vulnerabilities before the software developer has a chance to release a fix. Zero-day attacks can be highly effective and difficult to defend against.

Software vendors release patches and updates to address known vulnerabilities, but organizations must diligently apply these updates to maintain security. Attackers often target systems that have not been patched promptly, taking advantage of known vulnerabilities.

Exploiting software vulnerabilities typically involves a multi-step process. The attacker first identifies a target with specific software or configurations. They then search for vulnerabilities in the target, either through publicly available information or by conducting their research. Once a vulnerability is identified, the attacker crafts an exploit, which is a piece of code or a script designed to take advantage of the vulnerability.

Social engineering may also play a role in exploiting software vulnerabilities. Attackers may trick users into visiting malicious websites or downloading malicious files, which then exploit vulnerabilities on their systems. This underscores the importance of security awareness and user education.

The consequences of successfully exploiting software vulnerabilities can be severe. Attackers can gain unauthorized access to sensitive data, compromise the integrity of systems, disrupt operations, or even use compromised systems to launch further attacks. The impact on organizations can range from financial losses to reputational damage.

To defend against software vulnerabilities, organizations should adopt a comprehensive approach to cybersecurity. This includes regularly updating and patching software, implementing robust security measures, conducting vulnerability assessments and penetration testing, and educating users about security best practices.

Vulnerability management programs help organizations identify and prioritize vulnerabilities in their systems. Patch management processes ensure that security updates are applied promptly to mitigate known vulnerabilities. Intrusion detection and prevention systems can help identify and block exploitation attempts in real-time.

Security awareness training for employees is a vital component of defense. Users must be educated about the risks of downloading files or clicking on links from unknown or untrusted sources. They should also be aware of social engineering tactics used by attackers.

Additionally, organizations can deploy security tools and practices such as firewalls, antivirus software, and intrusion detection systems to detect and block attacks. Network segmentation can limit the exposure of critical systems to potential attackers.

Furthermore, security researchers and ethical hackers play a crucial role in identifying and reporting vulnerabilities responsibly. Organizations often offer bug bounty programs to encourage responsible disclosure of vulnerabilities.

In summary, understanding software vulnerabilities and how attackers exploit them is paramount in the field of cybersecurity. Vulnerabilities can exist in various forms, and attackers use a range of techniques to take advantage of them. To defend against these threats, organizations must adopt a multi-faceted approach that includes patch management, vulnerability assessment, user education, and the deployment of security tools and practices. By staying vigilant and proactive, organizations can significantly reduce the risk of falling victim to software vulnerability exploits.

Chapter 9: Evading Detection and Covering Tracks

In the dynamic realm of cybersecurity, the subject of anti-forensics and data destruction emerges as a complex and often controversial area of study, where the techniques and tactics employed to evade digital investigations collide with the principles of data integrity and accountability. Understanding these concepts is essential, as they shape the landscape of digital investigations and influence the strategies employed by both attackers and defenders.

Anti-forensics refers to a set of techniques and methods used to undermine or obstruct digital forensic investigations. These techniques are employed by malicious actors to cover their tracks, erase digital evidence, and make it challenging for investigators to reconstruct events accurately. Anti-forensics can be employed in various stages of an attack, from the initial compromise to the post-incident cleanup.

One common anti-forensic tactic is the manipulation or destruction of log files. Log files are records generated by computer systems, applications, and network devices to track events and activities. Attackers may modify or delete these logs to eliminate evidence of their actions, making it difficult for investigators to trace their activities.

Another anti-forensic technique involves the encryption or obfuscation of data. Attackers may encrypt files, communications, or entire drives to hide sensitive information. Encryption can make it challenging for investigators to access and analyze data without the appropriate decryption keys.

Data destruction, often synonymous with anti-forensics, is the deliberate and permanent erasure or destruction of digital data. Attackers may use various methods to achieve this, such as overwriting data with random information or physically damaging storage media.

Secure deletion tools and techniques, like file shredders or disk-wiping utilities, can be employed to ensure that data is unrecoverable. These tools go beyond simply deleting files and aim to overwrite the data multiple times, making it virtually impossible to retrieve.

The concept of anti-forensics raises ethical and legal questions, as it can be used not only by malicious actors but also by individuals or organizations seeking to protect their privacy or data. It is essential to differentiate between legitimate uses of data protection tools and malicious attempts to cover up illegal activities.

Forensic investigators employ a range of methods and technologies to overcome anti-forensic tactics and recover digital evidence. They may use specialized software and hardware tools to access and analyze data that has been intentionally concealed or encrypted. Additionally, investigators rely on their knowledge and expertise to uncover traces of anti-forensic activity.

Anti-forensics is not limited to digital techniques alone. It can also extend to physical actions, such as the destruction of hardware or the disposal of storage media. Attackers may physically damage computer components, burn or shred storage devices, or submerge them in water to prevent data recovery.

The impact of anti-forensics on digital investigations is significant. It can delay investigations, lead to incomplete findings, or result in the loss of crucial evidence. As a result, digital forensic experts continuously adapt their methodologies and tools to counter anti-forensic tactics effectively.

Data destruction is a closely related topic, as it often goes hand in hand with anti-forensics. While anti-forensics focuses on evading or obstructing investigations, data destruction centers on permanently eliminating data to prevent its recovery. Secure data destruction is a legitimate practice in cases where organizations need to dispose of sensitive information securely, such as customer records or intellectual property.

However, secure data destruction also carries responsibilities. Organizations must comply with data protection laws and regulations that govern the proper handling and disposal of data. Failing to do so can result in legal consequences and reputational damage.

One common method of secure data destruction is degaussing, which involves using strong magnetic fields to erase data from magnetic storage devices like hard drives and tapes. Degaussing renders the data irretrievable and is often used in highly sensitive environments.

Physical destruction of storage media is another secure data destruction method. This can include shredding, incineration, or disintegration of media to ensure that no data remnants remain. Physical destruction is particularly effective when dealing with optical media like CDs and DVDs.

Data sanitization, which involves overwriting data with random patterns, is a secure data destruction method commonly used for hard drives and solid-state drives. Properly executed data sanitization makes it nearly impossible to recover the original data.

Secure data destruction is a critical component of data lifecycle management. It ensures that data is disposed of securely when it is no longer needed, reducing the risk of data breaches and unauthorized access.

In summary, anti-forensics and data destruction are complex topics in the realm of cybersecurity and digital investigations. Anti-forensics encompasses techniques used to obstruct or evade digital forensic investigations, while data destruction involves the permanent elimination of digital data. While both have legitimate uses, it is essential to balance privacy and data protection with the need for accountability and security. Digital forensic experts continually adapt their methods to counter anti-forensic tactics, and organizations must comply with legal and ethical standards when handling and disposing of data.

In the ever-evolving landscape of cybersecurity, the concepts of tunneling and anonymity networks play a pivotal role, enabling individuals and organizations to protect their online privacy and security in an increasingly interconnected world. Understanding these topics is essential in navigating the digital realm and safeguarding sensitive information.

Tunneling, in the context of computer networking, refers to the practice of encapsulating one network protocol within another, effectively creating a secure and private communication channel over an otherwise untrusted or public network. This technique is used to ensure the confidentiality and integrity of data transmitted between two endpoints.

One common use case for tunneling is in virtual private networks (VPNs), which establish secure connections over the internet. VPNs create encrypted tunnels between the user's device and a remote server, allowing data to traverse the public internet while remaining protected from eavesdropping or interception. This is particularly valuable for remote workers or individuals seeking to browse the internet anonymously.

The Secure Sockets Layer (SSL) and its successor, Transport Layer Security (TLS), are widely used protocols for creating secure tunnels over the internet. SSL/TLS encryption ensures that data exchanged between a user's web browser and a website's server remains confidential and secure.

Another tunneling protocol is the Point-to-Point Tunneling Protocol (PPTP), which is commonly employed in VPN services. PPTP establishes secure connections for remote access to corporate networks or internet browsing, ensuring data privacy and security.

In addition to VPNs, tunneling can be used for secure file transfers, remote desktop connections, and other networked applications. By encapsulating data within secure tunnels, organizations can protect sensitive information from potential threats on the internet.

Anonymity networks, on the other hand, are designed to provide individuals with online anonymity by concealing their identity, location, and browsing habits. These networks are instrumental in safeguarding privacy and protecting against surveillance in an age where online activities are constantly monitored.

The Tor network, short for The Onion Router, is one of the most well-known anonymity networks. Tor operates by routing internet traffic through a series of volunteer-operated servers known as nodes. Each node decrypts a layer of encryption, revealing the next node in the path. This layered approach to routing makes it challenging for anyone, including government agencies and cybercriminals, to trace internet traffic back to its source.

Tor is commonly used by individuals who require high levels of online privacy and anonymity, such as whistleblowers, journalists, and activists living in repressive regimes. However, it also has legitimate uses, allowing users to browse the internet without revealing their identity or location.

I2P, or the Invisible Internet Project, is another anonymity network that focuses on secure and anonymous communication. I2P enables users to access websites, send emails, and chat anonymously within the network. It achieves this by routing traffic through a distributed network of peers, making it difficult for outsiders to determine the source or destination of data.

Freenet is a decentralized network that prioritizes censorship resistance and the protection of free speech. Freenet users can publish content, share files, and browse websites without revealing their identity. Content on Freenet is distributed across multiple nodes, ensuring that it remains accessible even if individual nodes are taken offline.

Anonymity networks like Tor, I2P, and Freenet are not without controversy. While they offer essential privacy protections, they can also be used for illicit activities, such as accessing the dark web or engaging in cybercrime.

Balancing the legitimate need for online privacy with the challenges posed by criminal activity remains a complex issue.

When using anonymity networks, it is crucial to remember that they are not foolproof. While they provide a high degree of privacy and security, they do not make users completely immune to all threats. Users should still exercise caution when sharing personal information or engaging in risky online behavior.

In summary, tunneling and anonymity networks are integral components of modern cybersecurity, enabling individuals and organizations to protect their online privacy and security. Tunneling protocols like VPNs and SSL/TLS create secure communication channels, while anonymity networks like Tor, I2P, and Freenet provide users with the means to browse the internet and communicate anonymously. However, it is essential to strike a balance between privacy rights and the need for security and accountability in the digital age. By understanding these concepts, individuals can make informed decisions about how to protect their online activities and information.

Chapter 10: Reporting and Post-Attack Analysis

In the realm of red team operations, documenting findings is a crucial step in the process, serving as the bridge that connects the execution of simulated attacks with the valuable insights gained from these exercises. Properly documenting red team findings is essential for ensuring that the results are comprehensible, actionable, and can lead to meaningful improvements in an organization's security posture.

When a red team engages in an assessment or penetration test, their primary objective is to simulate real-world attack scenarios, probing the defenses of an organization's systems, networks, and applications. Throughout the course of these activities, the red team uncovers vulnerabilities, weaknesses, and potential security gaps.

Effective documentation of these findings starts with meticulous record-keeping. Red team members must maintain detailed logs of their actions, including the tools used, techniques employed, and the systems or applications targeted. These logs provide a chronological account of the assessment and can be crucial in later stages of analysis and reporting.

In addition to logs, screenshots and recordings of key actions and discoveries are valuable documentation assets. Visual evidence helps illustrate the severity of findings and provides context for those reviewing the report. For example, capturing a screenshot of a successful exploitation of a vulnerability can be a powerful piece of documentation.

As the red team progresses, they should categorize and prioritize their findings based on their impact and potential risk to the organization. High-risk findings, such as critical vulnerabilities that could lead to data breaches or system compromise, should receive immediate attention and thorough documentation. Medium and low-risk findings, while still important, may be addressed with less urgency.

Each documented finding should include essential details, such as the specific vulnerability or weakness identified, its location (e.g., IP address or URL), the method of discovery, and any relevant evidence. Furthermore, findings should be categorized by severity, which can help organizations allocate resources and prioritize remediation efforts effectively.

Clear and concise descriptions of findings are essential. Red team reports should avoid technical jargon and acronyms that may be unfamiliar to non-technical stakeholders. Instead, findings should be presented in plain language that is easily understandable by executives and decision-makers.

To enhance the value of red team findings, they should be accompanied by recommended remediation actions. The red team's objective is not solely to identify weaknesses but also to provide guidance on how to address them effectively. Remediation recommendations should be practical, actionable, and tailored to the organization's specific environment and constraints.

In addition to detailing the technical aspects of findings, red team documentation should include a narrative that provides context and explains the potential impact of each discovery. This narrative helps stakeholders understand the real-world implications of the findings and the risks they pose to the organization.

Beyond individual findings, red team documentation should encompass a comprehensive executive summary that highlights key takeaways, overall risk assessment, and suggested security improvements. This executive summary serves as the primary communication tool for conveying the impact of the assessment to organizational leadership.

When presenting red team findings, it is essential to engage with stakeholders effectively. Meetings or presentations with technical teams, security personnel, and executives can provide an opportunity to discuss findings, answer questions, and ensure a clear understanding of the assessment's results.

In some cases, red team findings may require immediate action, such as patching critical vulnerabilities or addressing security misconfigurations. Rapid communication of these findings to relevant teams is crucial to mitigate potential risks promptly.

As part of the documentation process, red team members should collaborate with blue teams or defenders within the organization. Sharing findings and insights with the internal security team fosters a cooperative approach to addressing vulnerabilities and improving security posture. It also enables the blue team to gain a better understanding of the organization's specific challenges and areas of improvement.

Throughout the documentation and reporting process, maintaining confidentiality and security is paramount. Red team findings may include sensitive information, and the reports themselves can be valuable targets for attackers. Ensuring that documentation is securely stored and transmitted is essential to prevent unauthorized access or disclosure.

Finally, the documentation of red team findings serves as the foundation for continuous improvement. Organizations should use these findings as a roadmap for enhancing their security defenses, strengthening their incident response capabilities, and refining their security policies and procedures.

In summary, documenting red team findings is a critical aspect of red team operations. Effective documentation encompasses meticulous record-keeping, clear and concise descriptions of findings, prioritization based on risk, remediation recommendations, context-rich narratives, and executive summaries. Collaboration with internal security teams and timely communication of critical findings are also essential components. Ultimately, the goal of documenting red team findings is to provide organizations with actionable insights to enhance their security posture and protect against real-world threats.

In the world of red team operations, the culmination of an assessment or penetration test often leads to a critical phase: reflecting on the lessons learned and formulating improvement recommendations. This stage is pivotal in leveraging the insights gained during the engagement to enhance an organization's overall security posture.

Every red team engagement yields a wealth of information, from vulnerabilities and weaknesses in the security infrastructure to potential improvements in incident response and security awareness. The first step in this process is to comprehensively review the documentation of findings and the assessment's execution.

Through this review, the red team can identify patterns and trends in the vulnerabilities discovered. They can discern whether certain types of vulnerabilities are consistently present or if specific security controls consistently fail to deter attacks. This analysis is invaluable in identifying systemic weaknesses that may require targeted remediation efforts.

The red team should also consider the organization's response to simulated attacks. Were detection and incident response capabilities effective in identifying and mitigating threats promptly? Were there any blind spots or delays in recognizing the red team's activities? Evaluating the effectiveness of these processes can lead to improvements in the organization's defensive capabilities.

One of the key lessons learned often revolves around the human element of security. Social engineering and phishing attacks are common tactics used by red teams, and their success or failure provides insights into the organization's security culture and the effectiveness of security awareness training. Identifying areas where employees may be susceptible to manipulation or deception can guide targeted training efforts.

In addition to technical vulnerabilities and human factors, red team engagements may uncover shortcomings in security policies and procedures. These could include issues related to access control, data classification, incident response plans, and security documentation. Evaluating these aspects can lead to recommendations for refining policies and enhancing security procedures.

An essential aspect of lessons learned is understanding the impact of findings in the context of the organization's business objectives. Not all vulnerabilities are created equal, and their significance may vary based on potential consequences and business priorities. The red team should work closely with organizational stakeholders to assess the criticality of findings and prioritize remediation efforts accordingly.

Improvement recommendations should be framed in a way that emphasizes practicality and feasibility. They should provide clear guidance on how to address identified vulnerabilities, weaknesses, or gaps in security. Recommendations should be tailored to the organization's specific environment, taking into account its size, industry, regulatory requirements, and risk tolerance.

Furthermore, recommendations should consider the organization's available resources and budget constraints. While it's essential to identify ideal security improvements, it's equally important to propose realistic and achievable solutions that align with the organization's capabilities.

A collaborative approach is often beneficial in this phase, involving not only the red team but also the organization's internal security and IT teams. Working together ensures that recommendations are well-received, feasible to implement, and aligned with the organization's strategic objectives.

When presenting improvement recommendations, it's essential to convey the potential benefits and risks associated with each recommendation. Decision-makers within the organization need a clear understanding of the rationale behind each proposal, as well as the potential impact on security, operations, and compliance.

Furthermore, recommendations should align with a broader security roadmap or strategy. They should contribute to the organization's long-term goals for enhancing its security posture. This strategic alignment ensures that security improvements are not ad hoc but part of a comprehensive plan.

Tracking and monitoring progress on implementing improvement recommendations is a critical aspect of the post-engagement phase. Organizations should establish metrics and key performance indicators (KPIs) to measure the effectiveness of security enhancements over time. Regular reviews and assessments can help ensure that security measures remain effective and adaptive to evolving threats.

Finally, it's essential to maintain a culture of continuous improvement. Red team engagements should not be viewed as isolated events but as part of an ongoing effort to enhance security. Lessons learned and improvement recommendations from each engagement should feed into future security strategies and initiatives.

In summary, lessons learned and improvement recommendations are integral to the value of red team operations. They allow organizations to leverage the insights gained during assessments to strengthen their security posture. By comprehensively reviewing findings, assessing the effectiveness of security controls and procedures, and proposing practical recommendations, organizations can proactively address vulnerabilities, improve incident response, and maintain a robust security stance. Collaboration, strategic alignment, and a commitment to continuous improvement are key drivers in this phase of the red team engagement process.

BOOK 2
UNLOCKING THE BLACK BOX
ADVANCED TECHNIQUES IN ETHICAL HACKING
ROB BOTWRIGHT

Chapter 1: Advanced Hacking Methodologies

In the ever-evolving landscape of cybersecurity, understanding the Cyber Kill Chain model is essential for organizations seeking to defend against increasingly sophisticated cyber threats. The Cyber Kill Chain model is a framework that provides insights into the stages of a cyber attack, enabling organizations to detect and mitigate threats at various points in the attack lifecycle.

The concept of the Cyber Kill Chain was developed by defense contractor Lockheed Martin to describe the stages that adversaries typically go through when executing a cyber attack. The model consists of seven distinct stages, each representing a phase in the attacker's plan to infiltrate a target's network, compromise systems, and achieve their objectives.

The first stage of the Cyber Kill Chain is reconnaissance, where attackers gather information about their target. This can involve scanning for vulnerabilities, identifying potential entry points, and researching the target's employees and systems. Reconnaissance is often an initial step for threat actors to understand the target's weaknesses and devise an attack strategy.

The second stage is weaponization, where attackers create or acquire malicious tools and payloads designed to exploit vulnerabilities in the target's systems. These weapons may include malware, exploits, or phishing emails containing malicious attachments.

Weaponization is the preparation phase, where attackers craft their attack vector.

Delivery is the third stage, where attackers deliver their malicious payload to the target. This can occur through various means, such as email attachments, compromised websites, or social engineering tactics. Once the payload reaches the target's network or device, it is executed, initiating the attack.

The fourth stage is exploitation, where attackers leverage the vulnerabilities in the target's systems or applications to gain unauthorized access. This often involves executing malicious code or taking advantage of software flaws. Successful exploitation allows attackers to establish a foothold in the target's environment.

The fifth stage is installation, where attackers establish a persistent presence within the target's network. This may involve deploying additional malware, creating backdoors, or manipulating system settings to ensure continued access even if the initial compromise is detected and remediated.

Command and control (C2) is the sixth stage, where attackers establish communication channels with the compromised systems. This allows them to send instructions, receive data, and maintain control over the compromised environment. C2 mechanisms can be hidden within legitimate network traffic to evade detection.

The final stage of the Cyber Kill Chain is actions on objectives. In this phase, attackers pursue their ultimate goals, which may include data theft, espionage, disruption, or financial gain. The actions taken at this stage can vary widely, depending on the attacker's motives and the target's assets.

Understanding the Cyber Kill Chain model enables organizations to adopt a proactive approach to cybersecurity. By identifying and disrupting an attack at an early stage, organizations can prevent adversaries from reaching their ultimate objectives. This approach is more effective and cost-efficient than solely focusing on post-breach remediation.

To counter cyber threats effectively, organizations can implement security measures and controls at multiple points along the Cyber Kill Chain. For example, robust perimeter defenses, email filtering, and user awareness training can help thwart attacks in the reconnaissance and weaponization stages. Patch management and vulnerability scanning can address vulnerabilities before they are exploited.

Intrusion detection and prevention systems (IDS/IPS) play a vital role in detecting and blocking attacks during the delivery, exploitation, and installation stages. These systems can identify suspicious or malicious network traffic and trigger alerts or automatic responses to disrupt ongoing attacks.

Endpoint protection solutions, including antivirus and endpoint detection and response (EDR) tools, can help detect and mitigate attacks at the installation, C2, and actions on objectives stages. These solutions monitor endpoints for signs of compromise and can isolate or remediate affected systems.

Security information and event management (SIEM) systems are crucial for aggregating and analyzing data from various security controls to identify patterns and anomalies indicative of an ongoing attack. SIEM solutions enable security teams to respond quickly and effectively to threats.

Threat intelligence feeds and sharing platforms can provide organizations with up-to-date information about emerging threats, attacker tactics, and indicators of compromise (IOCs). By incorporating threat intelligence into their defenses, organizations can enhance their ability to detect and respond to threats aligned with the Cyber Kill Chain model.

Cyber threat hunting is an advanced security practice that involves actively seeking out and identifying threats within an organization's network. Threat hunters use their expertise and specialized tools to proactively search for signs of malicious activity, focusing on stages such as installation, C2, and actions on objectives.

In summary, the Cyber Kill Chain model offers a valuable framework for understanding the stages of a cyber attack and implementing proactive cybersecurity measures. By identifying and disrupting threats at various points along the Kill Chain, organizations can enhance their overall security posture and reduce the risk of successful cyberattacks. Adopting a multi-layered defense strategy that encompasses prevention, detection, and response is key to effectively countering today's evolving cyber threats.

In the realm of cybersecurity, understanding Advanced

Persistent Threat (APT) tactics is essential for organizations seeking to defend against some of the most sophisticated and persistent cyber adversaries. APTs represent a category of threat actors with highly developed capabilities and a long-term strategic focus on infiltrating target organizations, often with the goal of espionage, data theft, or disruption.

One of the defining characteristics of APTs is their persistence. APT actors are not interested in quick, opportunistic attacks. Instead, they employ a patient and methodical approach, often operating covertly within a target's environment for an extended period, sometimes months or even years. This persistence allows them to gather valuable intelligence and achieve their objectives stealthily.

To understand APT tactics, it's essential to delve into their modus operandi. APT actors typically initiate their campaigns with reconnaissance, gathering extensive information about the target organization. This reconnaissance phase may involve open-source intelligence (OSINT) gathering, domain registration lookups, and even social engineering tactics to acquire insider knowledge.

Once armed with intelligence, APTs move to the weaponization stage, where they craft customized and often highly sophisticated malicious tools and payloads. These may include advanced malware, zero-day exploits, and tailored phishing emails designed to target specific individuals within the organization. The level of sophistication and customization sets APTs apart from typical cybercriminals.

Delivery is the next stage, where APTs deliver their malicious payloads to target systems or users. This can occur through various channels, including email attachments, malicious websites, or compromised software updates. The delivery methods are carefully chosen to maximize the chances of successful infiltration.

After delivery, APTs proceed to the exploitation phase, where they leverage vulnerabilities in the target's systems or applications to gain a foothold. This often involves the use of zero-day exploits or the exploitation of known vulnerabilities for which patches are not yet available. This stage can be highly targeted, focusing on specific weaknesses within the organization.

Once inside the target environment, APTs focus on maintaining a persistent presence. They employ various techniques to evade detection, such as rootkits, anti-forensics tools, and advanced evasion tactics. This persistence enables them to remain hidden and continue their operations over an extended period, often bypassing traditional security measures.

Command and control (C2) is a critical aspect of APT operations. APT actors establish covert communication channels with compromised systems to issue commands, exfiltrate data, and receive instructions from their operators. These channels are designed to blend in with legitimate network traffic, making them difficult to detect.

The actions on objectives stage is where APTs pursue their primary mission. This can involve a wide range of activities, depending on the actor's goals. They may engage in data exfiltration, intellectual property theft, espionage, or disruption of critical systems. The actions on objectives stage represents the culmination of the APT's efforts and the achievement of their primary goals.

APTs are known for their adaptability and ability to evolve their tactics. They frequently update their malware and infrastructure to stay ahead of security defenses. This agility allows them to continue operating even after initial detection, making them particularly challenging adversaries.

To defend against APT tactics, organizations must adopt a multi-layered security approach. This includes robust perimeter defenses, such as firewalls, intrusion detection systems (IDS), and email filtering, to detect and block initial delivery and exploitation attempts. Patch management and vulnerability scanning are crucial to addressing known vulnerabilities that APTs might target.

Endpoint protection solutions, including antivirus and endpoint detection and response (EDR) tools, play a vital role in detecting and mitigating APT activity within the organization. These solutions monitor endpoints for signs of compromise and can help isolate or remediate affected systems.

Security information and event management (SIEM) systems are essential for aggregating and analyzing data from various security controls to identify patterns and anomalies indicative of APT activity. SIEM solutions enable security teams to respond quickly and effectively to APT threats.

Threat intelligence feeds and sharing platforms provide organizations with valuable information about APT tactics, techniques, and indicators of compromise (IOCs). Incorporating threat intelligence into security defenses allows organizations to proactively defend against known APT threats.

Cyber threat hunting is an advanced security practice that involves actively seeking out APTs and other threats within an organization's network. Threat hunters use their expertise and specialized tools to proactively search for signs of APT activity and take corrective actions.

In summary, understanding APT tactics is crucial for organizations seeking to defend against these persistent and highly capable adversaries. APTs employ patient, methodical, and sophisticated techniques to infiltrate and operate within target environments for extended periods. To counter APT threats effectively, organizations must adopt a proactive and multi-layered security approach that encompasses prevention, detection, and response. By staying vigilant and continuously evolving their defenses, organizations can reduce the risk of falling victim to APT tactics.

Chapter 2: Cryptography and Secure Communications

In the ever-evolving landscape of cybersecurity, encryption stands as a cornerstone of protecting sensitive data from prying eyes. Encryption algorithms and key management are fundamental components of this essential security practice, ensuring that information remains confidential, secure, and tamper-proof.

Encryption, at its core, is the process of converting plaintext data into ciphertext, making it unreadable without the appropriate decryption key. This cryptographic transformation serves as a powerful safeguard against unauthorized access, data breaches, and eavesdropping.

One of the primary considerations in encryption is the choice of encryption algorithm. Encryption algorithms are mathematical formulas or processes that determine how data is transformed from its original form (plaintext) into an unreadable form (ciphertext). There are various encryption algorithms available, each with its strengths and use cases.

One of the most widely used encryption algorithms is the Advanced Encryption Standard (AES). AES is a symmetric encryption algorithm, meaning the same key is used for both encryption and decryption. It is highly secure and efficient, making it suitable for a wide range of applications, from securing data at rest to encrypting data in transit.

Another commonly used encryption algorithm is RSA (Rivest-Shamir-Adleman), which is an asymmetric encryption algorithm. RSA uses a pair of keys, a public key for encryption and a private key for decryption. It is often used for securing communications and digital signatures.

Elliptic Curve Cryptography (ECC) is gaining popularity due to its strong security properties and efficiency, making it well-suited for resource-constrained devices and applications where computational overhead is a concern.

In addition to these algorithms, there are other symmetric and asymmetric encryption methods, such as Triple DES (3DES), Diffie-Hellman (DH), and various block ciphers and stream ciphers, each with its unique characteristics and applications.

Choosing the right encryption algorithm depends on several factors, including the level of security required, performance considerations, and compatibility with existing systems and standards. It is essential to assess these factors carefully to select the most appropriate algorithm for a specific use case.

Key management is another critical aspect of encryption. Encryption relies on cryptographic keys to lock and unlock data. These keys serve as the means to encrypt plaintext into ciphertext and decrypt ciphertext back into plaintext. Effective key management is essential to ensure the confidentiality and integrity of encrypted data.

Key generation is the first step in key management. Cryptographic keys must be generated securely and randomly. For symmetric encryption, where the same key is used for both encryption and decryption, key generation involves creating a strong, secret key that is kept confidential.

For asymmetric encryption, a key pair consisting of a public key and a private key is generated. The public key can be freely shared, while the private key must be securely safeguarded. The security of the private key is crucial, as it is used to decrypt data that has been encrypted with the corresponding public key.

Key distribution is the process of securely sharing cryptographic keys between parties. In asymmetric encryption, the public key can be openly distributed, but the private key must remain confidential. Secure channels or trusted authorities are often used to facilitate key distribution.

Key storage is a vital consideration in key management. Keys must be stored securely to prevent unauthorized access or theft. Hardware security modules (HSMs), secure key storage appliances, and cryptographic key vaults are used to protect cryptographic keys from compromise.

Key rotation involves periodically changing cryptographic keys to enhance security. Regularly rotating keys reduces the risk of key compromise and helps mitigate potential damage in case a key is ever breached. Key rotation schedules should be defined based on security policies and best practices.

Key revocation is the process of rendering a cryptographic key unusable. When a key is compromised or no longer needed, it should be revoked to prevent its misuse. Revocation mechanisms are essential to maintain the integrity of the encryption system.

Backup and recovery procedures are crucial in key management. Losing access to cryptographic keys can result in data loss or system downtime. Robust backup and recovery processes ensure that keys can be restored in the event of key loss or hardware failures.

Auditing and monitoring are essential for tracking key usage and detecting any unauthorized or suspicious activities related to keys. Key management systems often provide audit trails and logging capabilities to support these functions.

Encryption key management standards and best practices, such as those defined by the National Institute of Standards and Technology (NIST) and industry-specific regulations, provide guidance on key management processes and security controls. Organizations should adhere to these standards to ensure the effectiveness of their encryption implementations.

In summary, encryption algorithms and key management are foundational elements of modern cybersecurity. Encryption protects data from unauthorized access and ensures its confidentiality and integrity. Choosing the right encryption algorithm and implementing effective key management practices are essential for securing sensitive information in today's digital world. By carefully selecting encryption algorithms and following best practices for key generation, distribution, storage, rotation, revocation, backup, and monitoring, organizations can establish a robust security posture and protect their data from threats and breaches.

In today's interconnected world, secure communication protocols play a pivotal role in ensuring the confidentiality, integrity, and authenticity of data exchanged between parties. These protocols provide a framework for secure data transmission over networks, mitigating the risks associated with eavesdropping, tampering, and unauthorized access.

Secure communication protocols are designed to protect data while it is in transit between two or more entities. Whether it's sending confidential emails, making online purchases, or accessing sensitive information on the web, secure communication protocols are the invisible guardians that keep our digital interactions safe.

One of the most widely recognized secure communication protocols is Transport Layer Security (TLS). TLS, and its predecessor, Secure Sockets Layer (SSL), are cryptographic protocols that establish secure communication channels over the Internet. They are commonly used to secure web traffic, email transmissions, and various other network applications.

TLS employs encryption algorithms and digital certificates to ensure the confidentiality and integrity of data exchanged between a client and a server. When you see "https://" in your web browser's address bar, it indicates that TLS is being used to encrypt your connection, safeguarding your sensitive information during online transactions.

Another secure communication protocol frequently used for email is Pretty Good Privacy (PGP) or its open-source alternative, GNU Privacy Guard (GPG). PGP/GPG provides end-to-end encryption for emails, making it virtually impossible for anyone other than the intended recipient to decipher the message.

Secure Shell (SSH) is a protocol that ensures secure remote access and file transfers over an insecure network. System administrators and network engineers rely on SSH to connect to remote servers securely. SSH uses cryptographic keys to authenticate and encrypt data exchanged between the client and server.

Virtual Private Networks (VPNs) are another category of secure communication protocols that create encrypted tunnels for data traffic. VPNs are widely used to protect users' privacy and security when accessing the Internet, especially on public Wi-Fi networks. They provide anonymity and prevent eavesdropping by encrypting all data transmitted between the user and the VPN server.

Wireless networks also benefit from secure communication protocols, such as Wi-Fi Protected Access (WPA) and its successor, WPA2. These protocols ensure that data transmitted over wireless networks remains confidential and secure. Strong encryption and authentication mechanisms are used to prevent unauthorized access to the network.

For secure instant messaging and voice or video calls, Signal Protocol has gained prominence. Signal offers end-to-end encryption, making it challenging for third parties to intercept or decipher the communication. It is widely recognized for its commitment to privacy and security.

When it comes to securing financial transactions, the Payment Card Industry Data Security Standard (PCI DSS) enforces secure communication protocols for credit card processing. These protocols ensure the secure transmission of payment data between merchants and payment processors, reducing the risk of data breaches and fraud.

The Internet Protocol Security (IPsec) framework is used to secure communication at the network layer. IPsec encrypts and authenticates IP packets, providing a robust security layer for data transmitted across networks. It is commonly used in Virtual Private Networks (VPNs) and to secure data traffic between routers and firewalls.

In addition to these well-established secure communication protocols, newer ones are continually emerging to address evolving threats and vulnerabilities. Post-Quantum Cryptography (PQC) protocols, for instance, are being developed to safeguard data against the potential threat of quantum computers, which could break current encryption schemes.

Secure communication protocols are not limited to one particular application or technology. They span across various domains, from web browsing and email to file transfers and instant messaging. Their common goal is to protect the confidentiality of data, verify the identity of communicating parties, and ensure data integrity.

It's important to note that the effectiveness of secure communication protocols depends not only on the protocols themselves but also on their proper implementation and configuration. Even the most secure protocol can be compromised if not deployed correctly. This underscores the importance of keeping software and systems up-to-date with security patches and best practices.

Moreover, the use of strong cryptographic algorithms and key management practices is essential for the security of these protocols. Cryptographic keys must be generated securely, protected from unauthorized access, and regularly rotated to minimize the risk of compromise.

The role of secure communication protocols in cybersecurity cannot be overstated. They are the linchpin of secure online interactions, enabling individuals, businesses, and governments to exchange information, conduct transactions, and collaborate across the digital landscape. As the cyber threat landscape continues to evolve, the development and adoption of robust secure communication protocols will remain a cornerstone of effective cybersecurity strategies.

In summary, secure communication protocols are the invisible guardians of our digital interactions, safeguarding data against eavesdropping, tampering, and unauthorized access. These protocols, such as TLS, PGP/GPG, SSH, VPNs, and IPsec, serve as the backbone of secure online communications, ensuring the confidentiality, integrity, and authenticity of data transmitted over networks. Proper implementation, encryption practices, and key management are essential for the effectiveness of these protocols in today's evolving cybersecurity landscape.

Chapter 3: Exploiting Zero-Day Vulnerabilities

In the realm of cybersecurity, zero-days represent a unique and potent threat, challenging both defenders and attackers alike with their elusive nature and potential for devastating consequences. Understanding what zero-days are and how they are identified and exploited is essential in navigating the evolving landscape of digital security.

A zero-day vulnerability, often referred to simply as a "zero-day," is a software vulnerability that is unknown to the software vendor or developer. Unlike known vulnerabilities, for which patches or updates are available, zero-days are uncharted territory, offering no defenses against potential exploitation.

The term "zero-day" signifies that the vulnerability has zero days of protection since it is undisclosed, and there are no official fixes or mitigations in place. This vulnerability can be leveraged by attackers to compromise systems, steal data, or execute malicious code before the software vendor becomes aware of the issue and releases a patch.

Identifying zero-days requires a combination of skills, tools, and resources. In many cases, security researchers and ethical hackers actively seek out these vulnerabilities through a process known as "zero-day hunting." This involves scrutinizing software code, reverse engineering, and conducting extensive testing to discover unknown weaknesses.

Zero-day hunters often rely on techniques such as fuzz testing, which involves feeding an application with invalid or unexpected data to uncover vulnerabilities. This method can reveal unforeseen software flaws that could potentially be exploited by attackers.

Additionally, the security community benefits from responsible disclosure practices, where researchers or ethical hackers report zero-days to software vendors or organizations responsible for the affected software. This responsible disclosure allows vendors to develop and release patches to protect users from potential attacks.

On the flip side, malicious actors also engage in zero-day discovery, but with the intent to exploit these vulnerabilities for their gain. This creates a cat-and-mouse game between defenders and attackers, where the race is on to find and patch vulnerabilities before they can be exploited.

Once a zero-day vulnerability is identified, the next step is to exploit it. Exploitation refers to the process of taking advantage of a vulnerability to gain unauthorized access, execute arbitrary code, or carry out other malicious actions on a target system.

Exploiting a zero-day vulnerability typically involves crafting a malicious payload or attack code that can trigger the vulnerability when delivered to the target system. Attackers often create sophisticated exploits that can compromise a system with a high degree of reliability.

The choice of attack vector for zero-day exploitation depends on the nature of the vulnerability and the target environment. Common attack vectors include malicious email attachments, compromised websites, or specially crafted network packets.

In some cases, attackers may use social engineering tactics to trick users into unknowingly executing a malicious payload that triggers the zero-day vulnerability. This can involve convincing users to open seemingly harmless files or click on malicious links.

Zero-day exploits can have far-reaching consequences, from data breaches and financial losses to the compromise of critical infrastructure and national security. As a result, organizations must adopt proactive measures to protect against zero-day threats.

One essential aspect of defense against zero-days is the implementation of robust security practices, including network segmentation, intrusion detection systems (IDS), and endpoint security solutions. These measures can help detect and mitigate attacks leveraging zero-day vulnerabilities.

Furthermore, keeping software and systems up-to-date with the latest security patches is crucial. While zero-day vulnerabilities are, by definition, unknown to vendors, they may discover and patch these vulnerabilities over time as part of their security efforts.

The use of advanced threat detection technologies, such as behavioral analysis and anomaly detection, can help organizations identify suspicious activities that may indicate zero-day exploitation. These technologies can identify abnormal patterns or behaviors indicative of an ongoing attack.

The sharing of threat intelligence and collaboration within the security community can also play a vital role in defending against zero-day threats. Information sharing allows organizations to stay informed about emerging vulnerabilities and tactics used by attackers.

In summary, identifying and exploiting zero-day vulnerabilities represent a complex and dynamic aspect of the cybersecurity landscape. These undisclosed weaknesses in software pose a significant challenge for both defenders and attackers, as they are a double-edged sword that can be used for both security research and malicious purposes. To defend against zero-day threats, organizations must employ a multi-faceted approach that includes responsible disclosure, proactive security practices, advanced threat detection, and collaboration within the cybersecurity community. By staying vigilant and well-prepared, organizations can reduce the risk posed by these elusive vulnerabilities and minimize their potential impact.

Zero-day vulnerabilities, as we've discussed, are a cybersecurity nightmare, representing uncharted territory where attackers can strike without warning, and defenders are left scrambling to catch up.

Mitigating zero-day vulnerabilities is a challenging endeavor that requires a combination of proactive security measures, rapid response capabilities, and ongoing vigilance.

One of the fundamental strategies for zero-day mitigation is the implementation of strong access controls and least privilege principles. By limiting user privileges and access to essential resources, organizations can reduce the attack surface and make it more challenging for attackers to exploit unknown vulnerabilities.

Patching and updating software promptly is another key aspect of zero-day vulnerability mitigation. While zero-days are, by definition, unknown to software vendors, they may discover and patch these vulnerabilities over time as part of their ongoing security efforts.

The use of application whitelisting can be an effective defense against zero-day exploits. Whitelisting involves allowing only approved and trusted applications to run on a system while blocking all others. This limits the potential attack vectors available to attackers.

Network segmentation is a valuable practice to prevent the lateral movement of attackers who have exploited zero-day vulnerabilities. By dividing the network into isolated segments with restricted communication paths, organizations can limit the impact of an attack.

Intrusion detection and prevention systems (IDS/IPS) play a vital role in zero-day vulnerability mitigation. These systems can detect suspicious activities and known attack patterns, providing an early warning system that can trigger incident response actions.

Behavioral analysis and anomaly detection technologies can help organizations identify zero-day exploitation attempts. By monitoring user and system behaviors, these technologies can flag abnormal patterns indicative of an ongoing attack.

Continuous monitoring and log analysis are essential for identifying signs of zero-day exploitation. Security teams should closely examine logs and alerts for any unusual activities or indicators of compromise.

The importance of user training and awareness cannot be overstated in zero-day mitigation efforts. Users should be educated about the risks of social engineering tactics and the importance of not opening suspicious email attachments or clicking on unknown links.

Network and host-based firewalls can be configured to filter out known attack vectors and malicious traffic, reducing the risk of zero-day exploitation. Firewalls should be regularly updated with the latest threat intelligence feeds.

Regularly testing and auditing the security posture of an organization is essential for zero-day vulnerability mitigation. Vulnerability assessments and penetration testing can help identify weaknesses before attackers can exploit them.

Red teaming exercises, where simulated attacks are conducted by security professionals, can provide valuable insights into an organization's readiness to defend against zero-day exploits. These exercises can reveal weaknesses that need addressing.

Endpoint security solutions, such as advanced antivirus and endpoint detection and response (EDR) tools, can help detect and mitigate zero-day threats on individual devices. These solutions monitor endpoints for signs of compromise and can take action to isolate or remediate affected systems.

Security information and event management (SIEM) systems provide a centralized platform for aggregating and analyzing security data from various sources. SIEM solutions can help security teams detect and respond to zero-day exploitation attempts by correlating information from multiple security controls.

Collaboration within the cybersecurity community is a powerful weapon against zero-day threats. Information sharing and threat intelligence sharing platforms allow organizations to stay informed about emerging vulnerabilities and tactics used by attackers.

Bug bounty programs and responsible disclosure practices can incentivize security researchers and ethical hackers to report zero-day vulnerabilities to software vendors or organizations. This cooperative approach can help accelerate the development of patches and mitigate the risk posed by zero-days.

In summary, mitigating zero-day vulnerabilities requires a multi-layered and proactive approach to cybersecurity. While it is impossible to predict and prevent every zero-day exploit, organizations can significantly reduce their risk by implementing strong access controls, promptly patching and updating software, leveraging application whitelisting, and using intrusion detection and prevention systems. Behavioral analysis, user training, and regular testing and auditing are also crucial components of zero-day vulnerability mitigation. By staying vigilant and well-prepared, organizations can enhance their resilience against these elusive threats and minimize their potential impact.

Chapter 4: Advanced Network Scanning and Enumeration

Port scanning techniques are essential tools in the arsenal of both cybersecurity professionals and malicious hackers alike, enabling them to discover open ports and services on target systems, assess potential vulnerabilities, and gather valuable information for various purposes.

Understanding port scanning and the techniques involved can provide valuable insights into how networks and systems are probed and can help organizations defend against potential threats.

At its core, port scanning is the process of systematically scanning a target host or network to identify open ports and the services running on them. Ports are logical endpoints used for communication, and they allow different services or applications to listen for incoming connections.

One of the simplest and most widely used port scanning techniques is the TCP connect scan. In a TCP connect scan, the scanning tool attempts to establish a full TCP connection with the target port. If the connection is successful, the port is considered open, indicating that a service is actively listening on that port.

TCP SYN scanning, also known as half-open scanning, is another commonly used technique. In this method, the scanning tool sends a TCP SYN packet to the target port. If the port is open, it responds with a TCP SYN-ACK packet. If the port is closed, it responds with a TCP RST packet. By analyzing these responses, the scanner can determine the state of the port.

UDP scanning is used to identify open UDP ports on a target system. Unlike TCP, UDP is a connectionless protocol, making it more challenging to determine the state of UDP ports. Scanners typically send UDP packets to target ports and analyze responses to identify open UDP ports.

Stealth scanning techniques are designed to avoid detection by intrusion detection systems (IDS) or firewalls. One such technique is the TCP FIN scan, which sends a TCP FIN packet to the target port. If the port is closed, it should respond with a TCP RST packet. If the port is open, it may ignore the FIN packet.

Another stealthy technique is the TCP XMAS scan, which sends a TCP packet with the FIN, URG, and PSH flags set. The scanner then analyzes the response to determine the state of the port.

Idle scanning, also known as zombie scanning, is a technique where an attacker leverages an intermediary host to perform port scanning. By sending spoofed packets from the intermediary host and observing the responses, the attacker can identify open ports on the target system without revealing their own IP address.

Banner grabbing is a passive port scanning technique that involves connecting to open ports and collecting information about the service running on each port. This information can include service banners, version numbers, and other identifying details. Banner grabbing can help attackers identify specific vulnerabilities in services and applications.

Port knocking is a technique used to hide open ports from casual scans. In port knocking, a predefined sequence of connection attempts to closed ports must be made before the desired port is opened. This sequence is like a secret handshake that, when executed correctly, allows access to the intended service.

Firewalking is a technique used to determine which firewall rules are in place on a target network. By sending packets with increasing TTL (Time-to-Live) values, the scanner can infer which ports are allowed or blocked by the firewall based on the responses received.

Scanning tools, such as Nmap, are widely used by both security professionals and malicious actors for conducting port scans. These tools offer various scanning techniques, customization options, and reporting capabilities.

From a defensive perspective, organizations can employ several strategies to mitigate the risks associated with port scanning. Network intrusion detection systems (NIDS) and firewalls can be configured to detect and block scanning attempts. Regularly monitoring network traffic and analyzing logs can help identify suspicious scanning activities.

Port security measures, such as port filtering and access controls, can limit exposure to potential threats. Disabling unnecessary services and closing unused ports can reduce the attack surface and make it more challenging for attackers to find open ports.

It's also crucial to keep software and systems up-to-date with security patches, as known vulnerabilities can be targeted during scanning. Additionally, conducting regular vulnerability assessments and penetration testing can help organizations proactively identify and address potential weaknesses in their networks.

In summary, port scanning techniques are fundamental tools used in both offensive and defensive cybersecurity practices. Understanding these techniques and their implications can help organizations defend against potential threats, while security professionals can use them to assess and strengthen network security. By implementing security measures, monitoring network traffic, and staying informed about emerging threats, organizations can reduce the risk posed by port scanning and protect their valuable digital assets.

Banner grabbing and service enumeration are critical techniques in the field of cybersecurity, providing valuable insights into the services and applications running on target systems, their versions, and potentially identifying vulnerabilities or misconfigurations that could be exploited by attackers.

Banner grabbing, also known as banner grabbing or service fingerprinting, is the practice of connecting to an open network port on a target system and collecting information about the service running on that port.

When a network service or application establishes a connection with a client, it often sends a banner or response message to the client. This banner typically contains information about the service, such as its name, version, and sometimes additional details like the operating system it's running on.

Security professionals and ethical hackers use banner grabbing to gain insights into the target's infrastructure. They often use specialized tools like Telnet or netcat to connect to open ports and retrieve banners. The information gathered from banner grabbing can be crucial for understanding the target environment's security posture.

Service enumeration, on the other hand, involves actively probing a target system to identify the services running on various ports, as well as collecting detailed information about those services. Unlike banner grabbing, which focuses on a single port at a time, service enumeration aims to identify and catalog all available services on a target.

Service enumeration is typically performed using automated scanning tools, like Nmap or Nessus, that scan a range of ports on a target system and identify the services running on each port. These tools often perform version detection to determine the exact version of the service.

The information collected during service enumeration is valuable for several reasons. First, it helps administrators maintain an up-to-date inventory of the services and applications running in their environment. This is essential for effective asset management and security.

Second, service enumeration allows organizations to identify and address potential security vulnerabilities or misconfigurations in the services they run. By knowing the specific versions of services, administrators can prioritize patching or updating those that are known to have security issues.

Third, service enumeration helps in the creation of network diagrams and documentation. Understanding the network's service landscape is crucial for architects and administrators when designing and maintaining network infrastructure.

From an attacker's perspective, banner grabbing and service enumeration can be used to identify potential targets and gather information that could be leveraged in subsequent attacks. By knowing the services, versions, and potential vulnerabilities present on a target system, attackers can tailor their tactics to exploit weaknesses effectively.

To mitigate the risks associated with banner grabbing and service enumeration, organizations can implement several security measures. First, they can deploy intrusion detection and prevention systems (IDS/IPS) that can detect and alert on suspicious scanning activities.

Second, organizations should ensure that banners and detailed service information are not unnecessarily exposed to external networks. This can be achieved by configuring services to provide minimal information or by using application-layer firewalls to filter incoming traffic.

Third, strong access controls should be in place to restrict access to administrative interfaces and services. By limiting access to authorized personnel only, organizations can reduce the attack surface and minimize the impact of unauthorized scanning.

Regular vulnerability assessments and penetration testing can help organizations identify and remediate potential vulnerabilities discovered through banner grabbing and service enumeration. Security professionals can use the information gathered during these assessments to improve security controls and practices.

In summary, banner grabbing and service enumeration are essential techniques in both offensive and defensive cybersecurity strategies. They provide valuable insights into the services and applications running on target systems, aiding security professionals in assessing and improving security posture. While these techniques can be used by both defenders and attackers, organizations can employ security measures like intrusion detection, access controls, and regular assessments to mitigate potential risks associated with these practices. By staying vigilant and proactive, organizations can enhance their overall cybersecurity posture and protect against potential threats.

Chapter 5: Privilege Escalation and Post-Exploitation

Elevating user privileges is a critical concept in cybersecurity, one that involves increasing the level of access and control a user has within a computer system or network.

Typically, users are assigned specific levels of privilege or permissions that dictate what actions they can perform, what files they can access, and what system settings they can modify.

User privileges are essential for maintaining security and preventing unauthorized access to sensitive information or critical system functions.

However, there are scenarios in which users may need elevated privileges to perform certain tasks. For example, system administrators require elevated privileges to configure and manage systems, install software, and troubleshoot issues.

Elevating user privileges should be done cautiously and only when necessary, as it introduces security risks. Granting excessive privileges can make systems more vulnerable to exploitation by malicious actors.

Common methods for elevating user privileges include using administrator or root accounts, using privilege escalation tools, or leveraging vulnerabilities in the system.

One common practice for elevating privileges is using the administrator or root account, which has the highest level of access and control over a system. This account is typically used for administrative tasks and can perform actions that regular user accounts cannot.

However, it's crucial to limit the use of these accounts to authorized personnel and tasks that require elevated privileges. Using administrator or root accounts for routine activities can increase the risk of accidental system changes or malicious actions.

Privilege escalation tools are software programs or scripts that attempt to exploit vulnerabilities or misconfigurations in a system to gain elevated privileges. These tools are often used by attackers to gain unauthorized access to a system.

To prevent privilege escalation through vulnerabilities, organizations must keep their systems and software up-to-date with security patches. Regular patch management reduces the risk of attackers exploiting known vulnerabilities to elevate their privileges.

Another method of privilege escalation is through the abuse of misconfigurations or insecure settings in a system. Attackers may manipulate these settings to gain higher-level access.

To mitigate this risk, organizations should regularly conduct security audits and assessments to identify and correct misconfigurations. Implementing the principle of least privilege, which grants users only the minimum privileges they need to perform their tasks, can also limit the potential impact of privilege escalation.

In Windows environments, User Account Control (UAC) is a feature designed to prevent unauthorized elevation of privileges. UAC prompts users for confirmation when making changes that require elevated privileges, helping to prevent accidental or unauthorized privilege escalation.

In Unix-like operating systems, the sudo (superuser do) command allows authorized users to execute commands with elevated privileges. The sudoers file, which controls sudo permissions, should be configured carefully to restrict access to only authorized users and commands.

From a defensive standpoint, organizations can implement various security measures to detect and prevent privilege escalation attempts. Intrusion detection systems (IDS) and intrusion prevention systems (IPS) can monitor for suspicious activities or patterns indicative of privilege escalation attempts.

Endpoint security solutions, such as endpoint detection and response (EDR) tools, can help detect and mitigate privilege escalation attempts on individual devices. These solutions monitor system activities and can trigger alerts or take remedial actions when unusual behavior is detected.

Regular auditing and monitoring of user accounts, especially those with elevated privileges, are essential for identifying unauthorized privilege escalations. Security teams should review logs and audit trails to detect suspicious activities or access patterns.

In summary, elevating user privileges is a necessary but potentially risky practice in cybersecurity. It should be done sparingly, with careful consideration of security implications, and only for tasks that require higher-level access.

Mitigating the risks associated with privilege escalation involves implementing security best practices, keeping systems and software up-to-date, configuring access controls and permissions judiciously, and monitoring for unauthorized or suspicious activities.

By striking a balance between providing the necessary privileges for legitimate tasks and maintaining strong security controls, organizations can reduce the risk of privilege escalation and protect their systems and data from unauthorized access and manipulation.

Maintaining persistent access is a significant objective for attackers seeking to maintain a long-term presence within a compromised system or network.
It involves ensuring that unauthorized access is not only gained but also sustained over an extended period without detection.
Attackers pursue persistent access to achieve various malicious goals, such as data exfiltration, further exploitation, or maintaining control for future attacks.
One common method used by attackers to maintain persistence is the installation of backdoors or persistent malware on compromised systems.
Backdoors are hidden entry points or mechanisms left behind by attackers to provide them with ongoing access to a compromised system.
These backdoors are often concealed within legitimate-looking files or processes, making them challenging to detect.
Rootkits are a specific type of malware that attackers use to maintain persistent access. Rootkits are designed to hide their presence on a compromised system by modifying system files and processes at a deep level.
To maintain persistent access, attackers may utilize various techniques to evade detection and maintain control over the compromised system.
One such technique is stealthy communication with command-and-control (C2) servers. Attackers may use encrypted channels, such as HTTPS or DNS tunneling, to

communicate with their C2 servers, making it difficult for security controls to detect malicious traffic.

Persistence can also be achieved by creating scheduled tasks or cron jobs that periodically execute malicious code. This allows attackers to regain access to the compromised system even if their initial entry point is discovered and removed.

Some attackers employ rootkit-based persistence, which involves modifying the system's bootloader or kernel to conceal their presence.

Credential theft and privilege escalation are common tactics used by attackers to maintain persistent access. By stealing legitimate credentials or escalating their privileges, attackers can move laterally within a network and maintain control over multiple systems.

Fileless malware is another technique used for maintaining persistent access. This type of malware operates in memory without leaving traces on the file system, making it difficult to detect.

Attackers often focus on evading detection and maintaining a low profile to ensure their continued presence goes unnoticed.

Organizations must implement robust cybersecurity measures to detect and respond to persistent access attempts. This includes deploying intrusion detection systems (IDS), endpoint detection and response (EDR) solutions, and network traffic analysis tools.

Regular security assessments and vulnerability scanning can help identify and address weaknesses that attackers could exploit to maintain persistence.

Strong access controls, including the principle of least privilege (PoLP), can limit the ability of attackers to escalate privileges and move laterally within a network.

Timely patch management and software updates are essential to prevent attackers from exploiting known vulnerabilities to gain or maintain access.

Security incident response procedures should be in place to detect, investigate, and respond to indicators of persistent access. This includes analyzing logs, monitoring network traffic, and conducting threat hunting activities.

It's crucial to stay informed about emerging threats and attack techniques to anticipate and defend against persistent access attempts.

In summary, maintaining persistent access is a critical objective for attackers seeking to maintain control within compromised systems or networks.

Attackers employ various techniques, including backdoors, rootkits, stealthy communication, scheduled tasks, credential theft, privilege escalation, and fileless malware, to achieve and maintain persistence.

Organizations must be vigilant in implementing robust cybersecurity measures to detect and respond to persistent access attempts. This includes deploying intrusion detection systems, conducting security assessments, enforcing access controls, and maintaining a proactive incident response capability.

By staying one step ahead of attackers and continuously improving their security posture, organizations can reduce the risk of persistent access and protect their systems and data from long-term compromise.

Chapter 6: Advanced Web Application Attacks

SQL injection is a prevalent and potentially devastating cybersecurity vulnerability that occurs when an attacker exploits weaknesses in an application's input validation to manipulate a database query.

This technique allows the attacker to execute arbitrary SQL (Structured Query Language) statements against a database, potentially gaining unauthorized access, extracting sensitive data, or even modifying or deleting records.

SQL injection attacks often target web applications that interact with databases, and they can have severe consequences for organizations and their customers.

The fundamental principle behind SQL injection is the failure to properly validate and sanitize user inputs before incorporating them into SQL queries. When an application takes user inputs without adequate validation and directly inserts them into database queries, it becomes vulnerable to SQL injection.

Attackers can exploit SQL injection vulnerabilities by submitting specially crafted input data that includes malicious SQL code. This code is then executed by the application's database server, allowing the attacker to manipulate the query's behavior.

There are several types of SQL injection attacks, including classic or union-based attacks, blind attacks, time-based attacks, and out-of-band attacks.

In classic SQL injection, the attacker leverages input fields to inject malicious SQL statements that are concatenated with legitimate queries. The result is often a UNION query that combines data from different database tables.

Blind SQL injection attacks are more challenging to detect because they don't necessarily return data to the attacker's browser. Instead, the attacker relies on the application's behavior to infer the success or failure of the injected query. Time-based attacks, for example, involve delaying the application's response to gather information.

Out-of-band SQL injection attacks involve sending data to an external server controlled by the attacker, making them harder to detect since they don't rely on the application's response.

To defend against SQL injection, developers should adopt secure coding practices. Input validation and sanitization are crucial steps in preventing these attacks. Developers should use parameterized queries or prepared statements to separate user inputs from SQL code, making it nearly impossible for attackers to inject malicious code.

Web application firewalls (WAFs) are also valuable tools for mitigating SQL injection attacks. They can analyze incoming traffic and block malicious requests that attempt to exploit SQL injection vulnerabilities.

Database security measures, such as least privilege access controls and proper encryption of sensitive data, can further protect against potential SQL injection attacks.

Beyond SQL injection, there are other injection attack vectors that attackers may exploit, such as OS command injection and XML injection.

OS command injection occurs when an attacker manipulates an application to execute unauthorized operating system commands. This can lead to various malicious actions, including data exfiltration or system compromise.

XML injection attacks target applications that process XML data without proper validation and sanitization. Attackers can inject malicious XML content to manipulate the application's behavior, potentially causing data leakage or denial-of-service (DoS) attacks.

To defend against injection attacks in general, developers should follow best practices, such as input validation and output encoding, to ensure that user inputs are treated as data rather than executable code.

Additionally, regular security testing, including dynamic and static code analysis, can help identify and mitigate injection vulnerabilities in applications.

Web application firewalls (WAFs) and intrusion detection systems (IDS) can also assist in detecting and preventing injection attacks by monitoring and filtering incoming traffic.

In summary, SQL injection and similar injection attacks pose significant threats to web applications and databases, potentially leading to data breaches, unauthorized access, and system compromises.

To mitigate these risks, developers should implement secure coding practices, including input validation and the use of parameterized queries or prepared statements. Web application firewalls and security testing can provide additional layers of defense against injection attacks.

Furthermore, organizations should stay vigilant and informed about emerging threats and vulnerabilities to adapt their security measures accordingly and protect their valuable data and systems.

Cross-Site Scripting (XSS) is a pervasive web application security vulnerability that allows attackers to inject malicious scripts into web pages viewed by other users.

XSS attacks typically occur when an application includes untrusted data in the web page content that is then rendered by a user's browser.

Attackers can exploit XSS vulnerabilities to steal user credentials, session cookies, or other sensitive information, deface websites, redirect users to malicious sites, or perform actions on behalf of the victim.

There are several types of XSS attacks, including stored, reflected, and DOM-based XSS. Each type targets different aspects of web applications and poses varying degrees of risk.

Stored XSS occurs when an attacker injects a malicious script that is permanently stored on the target server. When a user visits a page containing the injected script, their browser executes it, allowing the attacker to steal data or perform actions on behalf of the victim.

Reflected XSS, on the other hand, involves the attacker tricking a user into clicking on a malicious link that contains the payload. The payload is then reflected off the web server and executed in the user's browser.

DOM-based XSS attacks manipulate the Document Object Model (DOM) of a web page to execute malicious code. This type of XSS is challenging to detect because it doesn't necessarily involve server-side code execution.

To defend against XSS attacks, developers must implement secure coding practices. Input validation and output encoding are essential to prevent untrusted data from being rendered as executable code.

Developers should also set the "HttpOnly" flag on cookies to prevent JavaScript from accessing sensitive session cookies, making it harder for attackers to steal them.

Content Security Policy (CSP) headers can be used to restrict the sources of executable scripts in a web page, mitigating the impact of XSS attacks.

Web application firewalls (WAFs) and security scanners can help identify and mitigate XSS vulnerabilities by inspecting incoming traffic for malicious payloads.

In addition to prevention, it's crucial to have a robust incident response plan in place to address potential XSS attacks. Rapid detection and remediation are essential to limit the damage caused by such attacks.

Beyond traditional XSS attacks, attackers may use various exploitation techniques to compromise web applications. These techniques include clickjacking, cross-site request forgery (CSRF), and session fixation attacks.

Clickjacking involves tricking users into clicking on hidden or disguised elements on a web page that perform actions they didn't intend. This can lead to unintended actions, such as making unauthorized transactions or changing account settings.

CSRF attacks force users to perform actions on web applications without their consent. Attackers exploit the user's authenticated session to execute actions like changing passwords or making financial transfers.

Session fixation attacks involve setting a user's session identifier to a known value, allowing the attacker to hijack the user's session.

To defend against these exploitation techniques, developers should implement security measures like anti-CSRF tokens, frame-busting scripts to prevent clickjacking, and secure session management practices.

Vulnerability scanning and penetration testing can help identify and remediate these types of vulnerabilities in web applications.

Beyond traditional web applications, attackers may also target Single Sign-On (SSO) systems, which provide users with a single set of credentials to access multiple applications.

Attackers may exploit SSO vulnerabilities to gain unauthorized access to multiple applications or impersonate legitimate users. Protecting SSO systems requires careful configuration and strong authentication measures.

In summary, Cross-Site Scripting (XSS) is a widespread web application vulnerability that allows attackers to inject malicious scripts into web pages viewed by other users.

XSS attacks come in various forms, including stored, reflected, and DOM-based XSS, each with its own characteristics and risks.

Developers must implement secure coding practices, input validation, output encoding, and Content Security Policy (CSP) headers to prevent XSS vulnerabilities.

Security measures like web application firewalls (WAFs), security scanners, and incident response plans are essential for detecting and responding to XSS attacks.

In addition to XSS, attackers may employ exploitation techniques such as clickjacking, CSRF, and session fixation to compromise web applications and SSO systems. Protecting against these attacks requires a combination of security measures and vigilant monitoring and response.

Chapter 7: Wireless and IoT Hacking

Wi-Fi penetration testing is a critical cybersecurity practice that assesses the security of wireless networks to identify vulnerabilities and weaknesses that could be exploited by malicious actors.

In today's connected world, Wi-Fi networks are ubiquitous, providing convenient access to the internet and local resources.

However, they also present significant security challenges, as unauthorized access to a Wi-Fi network can lead to data breaches, network compromise, and a variety of cyberattacks.

Wi-Fi penetration testing, also known as Wi-Fi security testing, is a proactive approach to uncovering and addressing these vulnerabilities before they can be exploited.

The process of Wi-Fi penetration testing typically involves a series of steps, starting with reconnaissance and information gathering. Testers gather information about the target network, including its SSID (Service Set Identifier), network architecture, and potential access points.

Once the information is collected, testers use various tools and techniques to assess the security of the network.

One common testing method is the use of wireless scanning tools to identify and locate Wi-Fi access points.

This helps testers understand the network's physical layout and identify potential entry points for attackers.

Testers also perform wireless signal analysis to assess signal strength and coverage areas, which can reveal areas with weak or no network protection.

Another crucial aspect of Wi-Fi penetration testing is testing for common security misconfigurations. This includes checking for default or weak passwords on network devices and ensuring that encryption protocols like WPA2 or WPA3 are properly implemented.

In addition to network device configuration, testers also assess the security of connected devices, such as wireless routers, access points, and IoT (Internet of Things) devices. These devices can introduce vulnerabilities if not adequately secured.

One of the primary objectives of Wi-Fi penetration testing is to identify and exploit vulnerabilities to gain unauthorized access to the network.

Testers may attempt to crack Wi-Fi passwords, bypass authentication mechanisms, or exploit weaknesses in encryption protocols. The goal is to simulate how an attacker might gain access to the network.

During the testing process, testers may also perform packet sniffing to capture and analyze network traffic. This can reveal sensitive information, such as login credentials or data transmitted over the network in plain text.

Wi-Fi penetration testing doesn't stop at identifying vulnerabilities; it also includes recommending remediation measures to strengthen the network's security.

This can involve suggesting changes to network configurations, recommending stronger authentication methods, or providing guidance on securing wireless devices and endpoints.

It's important to note that Wi-Fi penetration testing should be performed by trained and ethical professionals. Unauthorized penetration testing can disrupt network operations and potentially lead to legal consequences.

When conducting Wi-Fi penetration testing, it's essential to obtain proper authorization from the network owner or administrator. This ensures that the testing is conducted within legal and ethical boundaries.

In addition to ethical considerations, organizations should also be aware of compliance requirements related to Wi-Fi security testing. Some industries and regulatory bodies have specific guidelines and standards that organizations must follow when assessing their Wi-Fi networks.

Wi-Fi penetration testing is a continuous process, as both networks and attackers evolve over time. Regular testing helps organizations stay ahead of emerging threats and vulnerabilities.

In summary, Wi-Fi penetration testing is a crucial practice for assessing and enhancing the security of wireless networks.

It involves a systematic approach to identifying vulnerabilities, exploiting them to gain unauthorized access, and recommending remediation measures.

By conducting regular Wi-Fi penetration testing and following ethical and legal guidelines, organizations can strengthen the security of their wireless networks and protect against potential cyber threats.

The Internet of Things (IoT) has ushered in a new era of connectivity, where everyday objects and devices are equipped with sensors, software, and internet connectivity to gather and exchange data.

These IoT devices range from smart thermostats and wearables to industrial sensors and autonomous vehicles, and they have become integral to modern life and various industries.

However, the rapid proliferation of IoT devices has also given rise to significant security challenges, as many of these devices lack robust security measures.

IoT device exploitation refers to the practice of identifying and exploiting vulnerabilities in IoT devices to compromise their functionality, gain unauthorized access, or extract sensitive information.

One of the primary reasons IoT devices are susceptible to exploitation is their diverse and fragmented nature.

There is no universal standard for IoT security, and manufacturers often prioritize functionality and cost-efficiency over security measures.

This has led to a wide range of IoT devices with varying levels of security, some of which may have significant vulnerabilities that can be exploited by malicious actors.

To exploit IoT devices successfully, attackers typically follow a series of steps. The first step is reconnaissance, where they identify potential targets and gather information about the devices and their associated networks.

Once potential targets are identified, attackers may use various techniques to discover vulnerabilities in the devices. This can involve scanning for open ports, analyzing network traffic, or searching for known vulnerabilities in device firmware.

One common method for exploiting IoT devices is leveraging default or weak credentials. Many IoT devices come with default usernames and passwords that users may not change.

Attackers can scan for devices with default credentials and gain unauthorized access, often with full control over the device.

Another avenue of exploitation is firmware vulnerabilities. IoT devices run specialized software known as firmware, and vulnerabilities in this firmware can be exploited to compromise the device.

In some cases, attackers may also target the communication between IoT devices and the cloud or other networked resources.

Exploiting communication vulnerabilities can enable attackers to intercept data, manipulate device functionality, or launch attacks on other devices within the network.

IoT device exploitation is not limited to consumer devices. Industrial IoT (IIoT) devices, used in critical infrastructure and manufacturing, are also susceptible to exploitation.

Compromising IIoT devices can have severe consequences, including disruptions in manufacturing processes, damage to critical infrastructure, and safety hazards.

To defend against IoT device exploitation, organizations and users must take proactive measures.

One crucial step is ensuring that IoT devices are kept up to date with the latest firmware and security patches.

Manufacturers often release updates to address known vulnerabilities, and applying these updates promptly can mitigate exploitation risks.

Changing default credentials and using strong, unique passwords for IoT devices is another important practice.

Network segmentation can help isolate IoT devices from critical systems and data, limiting the potential impact of an exploitation.

Network monitoring and intrusion detection systems can also help identify unusual behavior or suspicious activities associated with IoT devices.

In addition to technical measures, user education is essential. Users should be aware of the security risks associated with IoT devices and follow best practices for securing them.

IoT device manufacturers must also prioritize security in their designs and implement robust security measures, including secure boot processes, strong encryption, and secure firmware updates.

The adoption of industry standards and security certifications can help ensure that IoT devices meet minimum security requirements.

Furthermore, regulatory bodies and governments are increasingly recognizing the importance of IoT security and may introduce regulations and standards to improve IoT device security.

In summary, IoT device exploitation is a significant cybersecurity concern as IoT devices continue to proliferate in our connected world.

Attackers exploit vulnerabilities in IoT devices to compromise their functionality, gain unauthorized access, or extract sensitive information.

To mitigate these risks, users and organizations must follow best practices for securing IoT devices, including regular updates, changing default credentials, network segmentation, and user education.

Manufacturers also play a crucial role in enhancing IoT device security through design and adherence to industry standards and certifications. As IoT continues to evolve, addressing its security challenges remains a priority for a safer and more connected future.

Chapter 8: Evading Advanced Security Measures

In the ever-evolving landscape of cybersecurity, attackers are constantly devising new techniques to evade detection and infiltrate systems.

Anti-virus and anti-malware software are crucial components of defense against malicious software and cyber threats.

These security tools are designed to detect and remove malware, such as viruses, Trojans, worms, and spyware, from computer systems and networks.

However, as security measures have improved, attackers have become more sophisticated in their attempts to bypass these protective layers.

Anti-virus and anti-malware bypass techniques involve strategies and tactics used by attackers to circumvent or defeat the detection capabilities of security software.

One common approach to bypassing these security tools is through the use of polymorphic malware.

Polymorphic malware is a type of malicious software that constantly changes its code and appearance, making it difficult for signature-based anti-virus and anti-malware solutions to detect.

Each time the malware infects a new system or is executed, it generates a slightly different version of itself, rendering traditional signature-based detection ineffective.

Another technique used to bypass anti-virus and anti-malware software is the use of encryption.

Attackers may encrypt their malicious code to conceal it from security scanners, making it appear as benign data. This encrypted payload is then decrypted and executed on the target system, allowing the malware to evade detection.

Similarly, attackers may use packers or crypters, which are tools that compress and encrypt malicious code, to obfuscate their intentions and defeat security software.

Additionally, attackers may employ code injection or code manipulation techniques to hide their malicious code within legitimate processes or applications.

By injecting malicious code into trusted processes or files, attackers can execute their malware without triggering alarms from anti-virus and anti-malware solutions.

Rootkit-based attacks are another avenue for bypassing security software.

Rootkits are a type of malware that can embed themselves deep within the operating system, allowing attackers to maintain persistent access to a compromised system.

These rootkits are often designed to evade detection by anti-virus and anti-malware software, as they can manipulate system calls and hide their presence from security scans.

Attackers may also exploit vulnerabilities in the anti-virus or anti-malware software itself to disable or subvert its capabilities.

This can involve exploiting known vulnerabilities in the software or using privilege escalation techniques to gain administrative access and manipulate the security software's settings.

Furthermore, attackers may use fileless malware, which operates solely in memory and leaves no traces on disk for traditional anti-virus and anti-malware tools to detect.

Fileless malware relies on scripts and system utilities to carry out malicious activities, making it challenging to identify through signature-based scans.

To defend against these anti-virus and anti-malware bypass techniques, organizations must adopt a multi-layered security approach.

This includes using advanced threat detection solutions that go beyond signature-based detection, such as behavior analysis and machine learning algorithms.

Regular software updates and patch management are essential to address vulnerabilities that attackers may exploit to bypass security software.

Security teams should also implement network segmentation to limit the lateral movement of malware within the network.

User education and awareness are critical components of defense, as many attacks rely on social engineering tactics to trick users into executing malicious code.

Finally, organizations should conduct regular security audits and penetration testing to identify weaknesses in their security posture and address them proactively.

In summary, anti-virus and anti-malware bypass techniques are sophisticated strategies employed by attackers to evade detection and infiltrate systems.

These techniques include the use of polymorphic malware, encryption, code injection, rootkits, and fileless malware, among others.

To defend against these threats, organizations must adopt a multi-layered security approach, implement advanced threat detection solutions, maintain up-to-date software, and prioritize user education and awareness.

Regular security audits and penetration testing are essential to staying ahead of evolving attack techniques and maintaining a strong defense against cyber threats.

Intrusion Detection Systems (IDS) are a critical component of network security, designed to detect and alert on suspicious or malicious activities within a network.

They analyze network traffic and system logs, looking for patterns and behaviors that may indicate an intrusion or security breach.

However, like many security measures, IDS is not foolproof, and attackers have developed various techniques to evade detection.

Intrusion Detection System evasion involves strategies and tactics employed by attackers to avoid detection by IDS and carry out their malicious activities undetected.

One common method of evasion is fragmentation, where attackers split malicious packets into smaller fragments that are transmitted separately.

IDS may have difficulty reassembling these fragments to detect malicious content, allowing attackers to bypass detection.

Another evasion technique involves protocol-based attacks, where attackers exploit vulnerabilities in the protocols used by IDS to interpret network traffic.

By crafting packets in a way that exploits these protocol vulnerabilities, attackers can deceive IDS and avoid detection.

Furthermore, attackers may employ encryption to hide their activities from IDS.

Encrypted traffic is challenging to analyze, as the content is concealed within the encryption layer, making it difficult for IDS to inspect the payload for malicious content.

To bypass IDS, attackers may also use evasion tools and techniques specifically designed to exploit vulnerabilities in IDS software.

These tools can manipulate network traffic in a way that confuses or overwhelms IDS, making it more likely to miss malicious activities.

Stealthy port scanning is another evasion technique where attackers scan for open ports on target systems without triggering IDS alerts.

By sending packets slowly and avoiding suspicious patterns, attackers can stay under the radar of IDS.

Attackers may also employ obfuscation techniques, such as encoding or encrypting their malicious payloads to make them appear benign to IDS.

Obfuscation makes it difficult for IDS to recognize malicious content and raises the chances of evasion.

Polymorphic malware, which constantly changes its code, can also thwart IDS detection.

With each iteration, the malware appears different, making it challenging for IDS to establish a consistent pattern for detection.

Signature-based IDS, which relies on predefined patterns or signatures to detect known threats, can be bypassed by zero-day attacks.

Zero-day attacks exploit vulnerabilities that are unknown to security vendors, and since there are no signatures to detect them, IDS may fail to identify the intrusion.

Furthermore, attackers may exploit evasion opportunities in the time gaps between signature updates.

Intrusion Detection System evasion requires security practitioners to employ advanced techniques and strategies to enhance detection capabilities.

One approach is to use anomaly-based IDS, which focuses on identifying unusual or suspicious behavior within a network.

Rather than relying solely on predefined signatures, anomaly-based IDS establishes baselines for normal network behavior and flags deviations from these baselines as potential threats.

Another tactic is to implement deep packet inspection, which allows IDS to analyze the content of network packets in detail, including encrypted traffic.

Deep packet inspection can uncover hidden malicious content that may evade other detection methods.

In addition to these technical solutions, security teams must stay vigilant and proactive.

Regular updates of IDS signatures and rules are essential to keep the system effective against known threats.

Security professionals should also conduct ongoing training to stay updated on emerging evasion techniques and enhance their ability to detect and respond to threats.

Collaboration and threat intelligence sharing within the security community can provide valuable insights into new evasion tactics and help organizations stay ahead of attackers.

In summary, Intrusion Detection System evasion is a significant challenge in the ever-evolving landscape of cybersecurity.

Attackers employ various techniques, including fragmentation, protocol-based attacks, encryption, evasion tools, and obfuscation, to bypass IDS and carry out their malicious activities undetected.

To counter these evasion techniques, organizations should consider anomaly-based IDS, deep packet inspection, regular signature updates, ongoing training, and collaboration with the broader security community.

By adopting a multi-layered approach and staying proactive, organizations can enhance their ability to detect and respond to evolving threats effectively.

Chapter 9: Advanced Social Engineering Tactics

Psychological manipulation and influence are powerful tools that can shape human behavior and decision-making in various contexts.

Understanding the mechanisms behind these techniques is crucial for both individuals and organizations to navigate the complexities of interpersonal relationships, marketing, persuasion, and even protection against manipulation.

Psychological manipulation involves tactics and strategies that exploit cognitive and emotional vulnerabilities in individuals to gain an advantage or control over them.

One common form of manipulation is emotional manipulation, where individuals use guilt, fear, or other emotions to influence someone's thoughts, feelings, or actions.

For example, a person might use emotional manipulation to make someone feel responsible for their unhappiness or to pressure them into complying with their wishes.

Another form of manipulation is gaslighting, where one person deliberately distorts or denies facts, events, or their own behavior to make another person doubt their perceptions and sanity.

Gaslighting can erode a person's confidence and self-esteem, leaving them vulnerable to further manipulation.

Social manipulation involves using social dynamics and interpersonal skills to influence others.

This can include techniques such as flattery, mirroring, and establishing rapport to create a sense of trust and connection.

Cults and extremist groups often employ social manipulation to recruit and retain members by isolating them from outside influences and reinforcing groupthink.

Persuasion is a form of influence that relies on rational arguments and appeals to logic, often using evidence and reasoning to convince someone to adopt a particular viewpoint or take a specific action.

Ethical persuasion seeks to inform and guide individuals toward choices that align with their best interests, while unethical persuasion may involve deception or manipulation of facts.

Marketing and advertising often use persuasion techniques to influence consumer behavior and drive purchasing decisions.

Understanding psychological manipulation and influence is essential for protecting oneself from being manipulated.

Individuals can develop critical thinking skills to evaluate information and claims critically, question their own beliefs, and recognize emotional manipulation tactics.

Moreover, setting clear boundaries and asserting oneself when necessary can help protect against manipulation.

In organizations and leadership, it's crucial to foster a culture of transparency, open communication, and ethical behavior to prevent manipulation and build trust among team members.

On the flip side, ethical use of influence and persuasion is an important skill in various aspects of life.

For example, negotiation relies on persuasive techniques to reach mutually beneficial agreements.

Effective leaders often use their influence to inspire and motivate their teams, driving them toward shared goals.

In marketing and sales, ethical persuasion can help customers make informed choices that benefit them.

Understanding the principles of persuasion, such as the reciprocity principle, commitment and consistency, and social proof, can empower individuals to make more persuasive arguments and decisions.

Psychological manipulation and influence can be used for both positive and negative purposes, depending on the intent and ethical considerations.

Ethical individuals and organizations prioritize transparency, honesty, and respect in their interactions with others.

Recognizing and safeguarding against manipulation while using influence and persuasion effectively are essential skills for navigating the complex social and professional landscapes we encounter in our daily lives.

Targeted spear phishing campaigns represent a highly sophisticated and dangerous form of cyberattack that focuses on specific individuals or organizations.

Unlike generic phishing attempts that cast a wide net in the hope of catching unsuspecting victims, spear phishing campaigns are meticulously crafted to deceive and manipulate specific targets.

The success of these campaigns often hinges on the attackers' ability to gather detailed information about their victims and create convincing and personalized messages.

In a targeted spear phishing campaign, the attackers typically begin by selecting their victims carefully, often with a specific objective in mind.

These objectives can range from stealing sensitive information like login credentials, financial data, or intellectual property to gaining unauthorized access to a network or system.

Once the targets are identified, attackers conduct extensive reconnaissance to gather as much information as possible about them.

This reconnaissance phase may involve scouring social media profiles, company websites, public records, and other sources to create a detailed profile of the victims.

Attackers look for personal information, work relationships, job titles, and any potential weaknesses or vulnerabilities that can be exploited.

With this information in hand, attackers can craft highly convincing and personalized phishing emails or messages.

These messages are designed to mimic legitimate communication and are often tailored to the victim's interests, job role, or even recent events in their personal or professional life.

Attackers may also spoof email addresses or domains to make their messages appear genuine, further increasing the likelihood that the victim will fall for the scam.

The content of spear phishing messages can vary widely, but common tactics include urgent requests for action, offers of enticing deals or opportunities, or notifications of security breaches or account issues that require immediate attention.

In some cases, attackers may use psychological manipulation techniques to create a sense of urgency, fear, or curiosity that compels the victim to take the desired action.

One prevalent form of targeted spear phishing is Business Email Compromise (BEC), where attackers impersonate high-ranking executives or trusted business partners to trick employees into making financial transfers or revealing sensitive information.

Another common objective is to deliver malware or malicious links that, when clicked or opened, infect the victim's device or network with malware.

To evade detection, attackers often use techniques such as fileless malware, which operates solely in memory and leaves no traces on the victim's system.

In some cases, attackers may conduct reconnaissance over an extended period, patiently waiting for the right moment to strike.

They may exploit specific events, such as corporate mergers, product launches, or financial reports, to increase the believability of their messages.

To protect against targeted spear phishing campaigns, individuals and organizations must be vigilant and implement robust cybersecurity measures.

One critical defense is user education and awareness training to help employees recognize phishing attempts and avoid falling victim to them.

Organizations should also implement multi-factor authentication (MFA) to add an extra layer of security, making it more challenging for attackers to gain unauthorized access.

Email filtering solutions and intrusion detection systems can help detect and block phishing emails before they reach the inbox. Furthermore, regularly updating software and security patches is essential to address vulnerabilities that attackers may exploit.

For individuals, it's important to be cautious about sharing personal information online and to verify the authenticity of email senders, especially when receiving unexpected or suspicious messages.

In summary, targeted spear phishing campaigns represent a sophisticated and highly effective form of cyberattack that focuses on specific individuals or organizations.

These campaigns leverage detailed reconnaissance to craft convincing and personalized phishing messages that aim to deceive and manipulate victims.

Defending against spear phishing requires a combination of user education, cybersecurity measures, and vigilance to recognize and thwart these carefully orchestrated attacks.

Chapter 10: Legal and Ethical Considerations in Ethical Hacking

Compliance and regulatory frameworks are essential components of the modern business landscape, shaping how organizations operate and ensuring they adhere to established standards and legal requirements.

These frameworks are designed to promote transparency, accountability, and the protection of various stakeholders, including customers, employees, and investors.

One prominent regulatory framework is the General Data Protection Regulation (GDPR), which governs the handling and processing of personal data for individuals within the European Union.

GDPR imposes strict requirements on organizations, such as obtaining explicit consent for data processing, providing individuals with access to their data, and notifying authorities of data breaches.

Non-compliance with GDPR can result in significant fines, making it crucial for organizations to implement robust data protection measures.

In the United States, the Health Insurance Portability and Accountability Act (HIPAA) is a key regulatory framework in the healthcare industry.

HIPAA mandates the protection of patient information, requiring healthcare organizations to implement safeguards to ensure the confidentiality and integrity of medical records.

Failure to comply with HIPAA can result in severe penalties, including fines and legal consequences.

Financial institutions are subject to regulatory frameworks like the Dodd-Frank Wall Street Reform and Consumer Protection Act, which aims to prevent financial crises and protect consumers.

Dodd-Frank includes provisions that increase transparency in financial markets, establish regulatory agencies, and impose stricter oversight of financial institutions.

Compliance with Dodd-Frank is essential for banks and financial firms to avoid legal and financial repercussions.

In the realm of cybersecurity, the Payment Card Industry Data Security Standard (PCI DSS) is a widely recognized compliance framework that applies to organizations handling credit card payments.

PCI DSS sets requirements for securing cardholder data, including encryption, access controls, and regular security assessments.

Non-compliance can result in fines, loss of reputation, and the revocation of the ability to process credit card payments.

Environmental regulations are crucial for protecting the planet, and organizations must comply with frameworks like the Kyoto Protocol, Paris Agreement, or local environmental laws.

These regulations set limits on greenhouse gas emissions, promote sustainable practices, and encourage the reduction of environmental impacts.

Failing to comply with environmental regulations can lead to legal penalties, damage to corporate reputation, and long-term ecological harm.

Compliance and regulatory frameworks are not limited to specific industries or regions.

Many organizations operate globally and must navigate a complex web of international, national, and industry-specific regulations.

To address this challenge, some organizations adopt a comprehensive approach to compliance management, establishing compliance teams, conducting regular risk assessments, and developing compliance policies and procedures.

Moreover, technology plays a vital role in compliance, with many organizations implementing software solutions to automate compliance monitoring, reporting, and documentation.

Compliance is not only a legal and regulatory requirement but also an ethical responsibility.

Organizations that prioritize compliance demonstrate a commitment to ethical business practices, transparency, and the well-being of their stakeholders.

Compliance can also lead to increased customer trust and confidence, as consumers are more likely to engage with organizations they perceive as trustworthy and responsible.

Furthermore, compliance with regulatory frameworks often enhances cybersecurity, data privacy, and risk management, reducing the likelihood of data breaches and financial losses.

In the context of cybersecurity, compliance frameworks like the National Institute of Standards and Technology (NIST) Cybersecurity Framework provide organizations with a structured approach to improving their cybersecurity posture.

NIST's framework consists of five core functions: Identify, Protect, Detect, Respond, and Recover.

By aligning with these functions, organizations can better assess their cybersecurity risks, establish security controls, and develop incident response plans.

Similarly, in the healthcare sector, the Health Information Trust Alliance (HITRUST) Common Security Framework (CSF) helps organizations address the unique regulatory challenges of healthcare data.

HITRUST CSF provides a comprehensive set of controls and requirements to safeguard healthcare information and ensure compliance with various regulations, including HIPAA.

In summary, compliance and regulatory frameworks are integral to the business world, shaping how organizations operate, manage risk, and protect their stakeholders.

These frameworks span various industries, addressing specific legal, ethical, and environmental requirements.

Compliance is not only a legal obligation but also a crucial element of responsible and ethical business conduct, promoting transparency, accountability, and trust.

By aligning with compliance requirements, organizations can enhance their cybersecurity, data privacy, and overall risk management, ultimately contributing to their long-term success and sustainability.

Responsible disclosure and bug bounty programs play a crucial role in the world of cybersecurity, fostering collaboration between security researchers, ethical hackers, and organizations to identify and address vulnerabilities.

These programs are essential components of a proactive approach to cybersecurity, helping organizations identify and mitigate potential threats before malicious actors can exploit them.

Responsible disclosure, also known as responsible vulnerability disclosure, is a structured process that allows security researchers and individuals to report security vulnerabilities they discover in an organization's software, systems, or services.

The primary goal of responsible disclosure is to ensure that vulnerabilities are reported to the organization in a way that allows them to fix the issue promptly and deploy necessary patches or updates.

In responsible disclosure, researchers typically follow a set of guidelines and ethical principles, such as providing organizations with a reasonable amount of time to fix the vulnerability before making it public.

This responsible approach minimizes the risk of the vulnerability being exploited by malicious actors while giving organizations the opportunity to address the issue.

Bug bounty programs are initiatives launched by organizations to incentivize security researchers and ethical hackers to actively search for and report vulnerabilities in their systems.

These programs offer financial rewards or other incentives to individuals who successfully identify and report security weaknesses.

Bug bounty programs have gained popularity in recent years, with many prominent companies and organizations, including technology giants like Google, Microsoft, and Facebook, offering such programs.

The concept behind bug bounty programs is simple: by offering rewards for vulnerability discoveries, organizations harness the collective knowledge and expertise of the security community to improve their security posture.

These programs encourage ethical hackers to actively seek out and report vulnerabilities, ultimately helping organizations strengthen their defenses.

Bug bounty programs typically have defined rules of engagement, including the types of vulnerabilities that are eligible for rewards, the scope of the program (e.g., specific websites, mobile applications, or services), and the reward amounts based on the severity of the reported vulnerabilities.

Common vulnerabilities sought in bug bounty programs include cross-site scripting (XSS) vulnerabilities, remote code execution (RCE) flaws, and data leakage issues.

One of the key benefits of bug bounty programs is that they create a direct line of communication between organizations and the security research community.

This open channel enables security researchers to report vulnerabilities directly to organizations, allowing for faster and more efficient resolution of security issues.

Additionally, bug bounty programs help organizations identify vulnerabilities that may have otherwise gone unnoticed or unreported, reducing the risk of data breaches and cyberattacks.

Moreover, bug bounty programs can enhance an organization's reputation by demonstrating a commitment to security and responsible disclosure.

However, for these programs to be effective, organizations must be prepared to respond promptly to vulnerability reports and provide appropriate rewards to incentivize researchers to participate.

While responsible disclosure and bug bounty programs offer many benefits, they also come with challenges.

One challenge is the potential for false or malicious reports from individuals seeking financial rewards.

Organizations must have processes in place to assess the validity and severity of reported vulnerabilities to avoid wasting resources on non-issues.

Another challenge is setting appropriate reward amounts that motivate researchers without overextending the organization's budget.

Finding the right balance between rewards and the value of the identified vulnerabilities is crucial.

Furthermore, organizations must have a structured and efficient process for triaging and addressing reported vulnerabilities to ensure timely resolutions.

In summary, responsible disclosure and bug bounty programs are integral to modern cybersecurity practices, enabling organizations to harness the collective expertise of security researchers and ethical hackers to identify and address vulnerabilities.

These programs foster collaboration, enhance security postures, and promote responsible and ethical approaches to vulnerability reporting.

While they come with challenges, organizations that implement these initiatives are better positioned to proactively protect their systems and data from potential threats.

BOOK 3
MASTERING THE ART OF SOCIAL ENGINEERING TACTICS
FOR RED TEAM PROFESSIONALS

ROB BOTWRIGHT

Chapter 1: The Psychology of Social Engineering

Cognitive biases are inherent patterns of thinking and decision-making that can influence our perceptions, judgments, and actions in various ways.

These biases are not necessarily a result of irrationality or lack of intelligence, but rather they are mental shortcuts that our brains use to process information efficiently.

Understanding cognitive biases is essential because they can lead to errors in judgment, decision-making, and problem-solving.

One common cognitive bias is confirmation bias, which is the tendency to seek out and favor information that confirms our existing beliefs and opinions while ignoring or downplaying conflicting information.

Confirmation bias can lead to a closed-minded approach and prevent us from considering alternative viewpoints or reevaluating our own beliefs.

Another prevalent cognitive bias is the availability heuristic, where our judgment is influenced by the ease with which we can recall examples or information related to a particular topic.

This bias can cause us to overestimate the likelihood of events that are more readily available in our memory, even if they are not statistically more probable.

The anchoring bias is another cognitive bias that occurs when we rely too heavily on the first piece of information (the "anchor") we encounter when making decisions, even if that information is irrelevant or misleading.

For example, when negotiating a price, if the seller suggests a high initial price, it can anchor our perception of what is a reasonable price, leading us to accept a higher cost than we might have otherwise.

The overconfidence bias is the tendency to overestimate our own abilities, knowledge, or the accuracy of our beliefs.

This bias can lead to overestimating our chances of success in a task or underestimating the risks involved, potentially resulting in poor decision-making and unexpected outcomes.

Another cognitive bias that affects decision-making is the sunk cost fallacy, which occurs when we continue to invest time, effort, or resources into a project or decision solely because we have already committed significant resources, even if it no longer makes sense to do so.

This bias can lead to poor resource allocation and a failure to cut losses when necessary.

The framing effect is a cognitive bias in which the way information is presented or framed can significantly influence our choices and decisions.

For example, a medical treatment described as having a 90% success rate may be perceived more positively than one described as having a 10% failure rate, even though they are functionally equivalent.

Cognitive biases can also manifest in group settings. Groupthink, for instance, is a bias that occurs when members of a group prioritize harmony and consensus over critical evaluation of ideas or decisions.

This can lead to suboptimal decisions as dissenting opinions are suppressed or ignored, and group members conform to the prevailing view.

The status quo bias is the inclination to prefer things to remain as they are and resist change, even when change might be beneficial.

This bias can hinder innovation and progress by discouraging individuals and organizations from exploring new ideas or approaches.

Anchoring bias, discussed earlier, can also affect group decision-making, as the first piece of information presented in a group setting can anchor the entire group's perception of a situation.

Cognitive biases are not necessarily negative or harmful in all situations. Some biases may serve as adaptive shortcuts that help us process information quickly in our daily lives.

However, it is essential to recognize and mitigate these biases when they have the potential to lead to errors or poor decisions.

Developing awareness of cognitive biases is the first step in managing and minimizing their impact.

By actively questioning our own thought processes, seeking diverse perspectives, and using critical thinking skills, we can make more informed and rational decisions.

In professional settings, organizations can implement strategies such as diversity of thought, decision-making frameworks, and peer review processes to counteract the influence of cognitive biases.

Furthermore, training programs and workshops on cognitive biases can help individuals and teams develop the skills to recognize and address these biases effectively.

In summary, understanding cognitive biases is a fundamental aspect of decision-making and critical thinking.

These biases are inherent in human cognition and can influence our judgments and choices in both positive and negative ways.

By recognizing these biases and actively working to mitigate their effects, individuals and organizations can make more informed and rational decisions, ultimately leading to better outcomes in various aspects of life.

Influence and persuasion techniques are essential skills in both personal and professional life, allowing individuals to effectively communicate, negotiate, and achieve their goals.

These techniques draw on psychological principles to influence the thoughts, behaviors, and decisions of others in a positive and ethical manner.

Understanding and applying these techniques can lead to more successful interactions and improved relationships.

One fundamental aspect of influence and persuasion is the principle of reciprocity, which suggests that people tend to feel obligated to reciprocate when someone does something for them.

By offering assistance, providing a favor, or showing kindness, individuals can create a sense of indebtedness in others, making them more likely to agree to requests or offers in return.

Another influential technique is social proof, which relies on the idea that people often look to the behavior of others to guide their own actions.

When individuals see that others have chosen a particular course of action or made a certain decision, they are more likely to follow suit.

For example, positive reviews and testimonials can be powerful tools in persuading consumers to purchase a product or service.

The principle of scarcity suggests that people tend to assign greater value to items or opportunities that are perceived as rare, limited, or in high demand.

By highlighting the scarcity of a product or the limited time available to take advantage of an offer, individuals can create a sense of urgency that motivates others to act quickly.

Likability is another influential factor in persuasion. People are more inclined to agree with and be influenced by individuals they like and trust.

Building rapport, finding common interests, and showing genuine appreciation can enhance likability and make persuasion more effective.

Reciprocity, social proof, scarcity, and likability are just a few of the many techniques used in influence and persuasion.

Authority is another critical factor, as individuals tend to be more persuaded by those perceived as experts or authorities in a particular field.

Citing credible sources, showcasing relevant credentials, and demonstrating expertise can enhance the persuasiveness of a message or argument.

Consistency is a principle that suggests people strive to be consistent in their words and actions.

Once individuals commit to a specific position or action, they are more likely to follow through and remain consistent with that commitment.

Therefore, gaining an initial small commitment from someone can increase the likelihood of obtaining a larger commitment later.

The concept of liking and similarity plays a significant role in influence. People are more likely to be persuaded by those they perceive as similar to themselves.

Building rapport and finding common ground can create a sense of connection and increase the effectiveness of persuasion efforts.

Reciprocity, consistency, authority, and liking are principles rooted in Robert Cialdini's influential book "Influence: The Psychology of Persuasion," where he identified these factors as key drivers of human behavior.

In the realm of negotiation, the art of persuasion often involves finding common interests and creating mutually beneficial solutions.

Negotiators use techniques such as active listening, empathy, and effective communication to understand the needs and concerns of the other party and find areas of agreement.

Additionally, the use of concessions and compromise can help bridge gaps and lead to successful negotiations.

Influence and persuasion techniques are also prevalent in marketing and advertising. Advertisers use persuasive messaging, emotional appeals, and social proof to encourage consumers to make purchasing decisions.

The use of testimonials, celebrity endorsements, and limited-time offers are common strategies to influence consumer behavior.

In the workplace, persuasion skills are essential for leadership and management. Leaders must motivate and inspire their teams to achieve common goals.

Effective leaders use techniques such as storytelling, vision casting, and leading by example to influence their employees positively.

In the context of sales, persuasion techniques are crucial for convincing potential customers to make a purchase.

Sales professionals often employ techniques like objection handling, building rapport, and presenting compelling value propositions to close deals successfully.

It's important to note that ethical considerations should always underlie the use of influence and persuasion techniques.

Manipulative or coercive tactics that exploit vulnerabilities or deceive others are not only unethical but can also harm relationships and damage reputations.

Ethical persuasion emphasizes transparency, honesty, and respect for the autonomy and choices of others.

To become more skilled in the art of influence and persuasion, individuals can seek out training, books, and courses that delve into the psychology and techniques of persuasion.

Practice and feedback are also vital for honing these skills.

Furthermore, self-awareness is crucial in recognizing one's own biases and tendencies in persuasion and adapting strategies to suit different situations and audiences.

In summary, influence and persuasion techniques are powerful tools for achieving personal and professional objectives.

Understanding the principles of reciprocity, social proof, scarcity, likability, authority, consistency, and others can enhance one's ability to persuade effectively.

However, the ethical use of these techniques is paramount, as ethical persuasion builds trust, fosters positive relationships, and contributes to long-term success in various areas of life.

Chapter 2: Building Effective Pretexting Scenarios

Creating convincing false identities is a complex and multi-faceted skill that has been employed for various purposes throughout history.

Individuals and organizations have used false identities for espionage, fraud, privacy protection, and even artistic expression.

While the idea of creating a false identity may seem mysterious and clandestine, it often involves a combination of research, storytelling, and attention to detail.

One common reason for crafting a false identity is the need for anonymity and privacy in an increasingly interconnected world.

People may wish to shield their personal information or activities from prying eyes, whether it's to protect their privacy, avoid unwanted solicitations, or maintain a sense of control over their online presence.

Creating a pseudonym or online persona can provide a layer of anonymity, allowing individuals to interact online without revealing their true identity.

For some, it's a matter of personal safety, especially in situations where revealing their real name or location could pose risks.

In the world of fiction, authors often create false identities for characters, inventing entire life histories, personalities, and backgrounds to bring their stories to life.

These fabricated identities serve as the foundation for compelling narratives and help readers engage with the characters on a deeper level.

In espionage and intelligence operations, the creation of false identities is a critical aspect of undercover work.

Spies and agents adopt new personas to infiltrate organizations, gather information, and carry out covert missions.

This often involves obtaining authentic identification documents, such as passports and driver's licenses, under the false identity.

The creation of these documents can be a complex and risky endeavor, as any inconsistencies or discrepancies could raise suspicions.

False identities are also used in the world of fraud and financial crimes, where individuals or groups may assume fake names and backgrounds to perpetrate scams, embezzlement, or identity theft.

These criminals often engage in extensive research to craft believable backstories and manipulate their victims.

In some cases, they may use social engineering tactics to exploit trust and gain access to sensitive information.

The creation of a convincing false identity typically starts with careful research.

This may involve gathering information about the desired persona's background, including birthplace, education, employment history, and family details.

Researchers may delve into historical records, public databases, and online sources to construct a plausible life story.

Attention to detail is crucial, as any inconsistencies or inaccuracies can cast doubt on the false identity.

Next comes the art of storytelling, where the creator weaves together the collected information into a cohesive and believable narrative.

This narrative should not only cover the basics of the false identity but also provide context and depth to make it more convincing.

For example, the creator may invent anecdotes, hobbies, and personal quirks that humanize the persona and make them appear more genuine.

Additionally, the creator must ensure that the false identity aligns with the target audience's expectations and cultural norms.

Different contexts and environments may require different personas, so adaptability is key.

For those who wish to maintain online anonymity, creating a convincing false identity can involve crafting a digital persona that aligns with their goals.

This might include using a pseudonym, creating a fictional biography, and even fabricating social media profiles.

Online personas can be used for various purposes, from participating in online communities without revealing one's true identity to expressing opinions or engaging in creative endeavors.

However, it's essential to remember that even in online interactions, ethical considerations should guide the use of false identities.

Engaging in online harassment, spreading misinformation, or conducting illegal activities under a false identity is both unethical and potentially illegal.

Moreover, platforms and websites often have policies against impersonation and fraudulent activities, which can lead to account suspension or legal consequences.

In espionage and undercover work, the creation of false identities requires a high degree of skill and meticulous planning.

Operatives must not only adopt new names and backgrounds but also learn to embody the persona convincingly.

This includes mastering the language, customs, and behaviors associated with the false identity.

Operatives may undergo extensive training to prepare for their roles, which can involve studying the culture and history of the target environment.

In some cases, they may work with experts to create realistic cover stories and documentation.

Maintaining the false identity can be challenging, as operatives must navigate complex situations, build trust, and gather intelligence while avoiding detection.

One small mistake or inconsistency can jeopardize an entire mission.

In the realm of fiction, authors often draw inspiration from real-life individuals who have successfully created false identities.

These stories of impostors and con artists have fascinated readers for generations, showcasing the creativity and audacity of those who can convincingly assume new personas.

In summary, the art of creating convincing false identities is a multifaceted skill that can serve various purposes, from safeguarding privacy to espionage and storytelling.

It involves research, storytelling, attention to detail, and, in some cases, mastery of language and culture.

However, it's essential to use false identities ethically and within the boundaries of the law, as the consequences of misuse can be severe.

Crafting believable scenarios is a valuable skill in various contexts, from storytelling and entertainment to business, education, and problem-solving.

A well-crafted scenario immerses participants or readers in a fictional or real-world situation, enabling them to explore possibilities, make decisions, and learn from their experiences.

Creating compelling scenarios involves combining elements of creativity, realism, and engagement to captivate the audience's attention and provoke thought.

In the realm of storytelling, authors use scenarios to shape the narrative and develop characters.

A scenario serves as the backdrop for the plot, influencing character decisions and actions.

Through scenarios, authors can explore themes, conflicts, and character development, drawing readers into the story's world.

In the business world, scenario planning is a strategic tool used to anticipate and prepare for different future outcomes.

Organizations create scenarios to assess potential risks, opportunities, and challenges they may face.

By considering various scenarios, businesses can develop contingency plans and make informed decisions that lead to more resilient strategies.

In the realm of education, scenario-based learning is a powerful pedagogical approach.

Educators use scenarios to engage students in real-world problem-solving, critical thinking, and decision-making.

These scenarios provide a context for applying knowledge and skills in practical situations, enhancing the learning experience.

Crafting believable scenarios begins with a clear understanding of the desired learning or storytelling objectives.

What do you want the audience to gain from the scenario, and what are the key takeaways?

Once the objectives are defined, the next step is to create a detailed scenario background.

In storytelling, this may involve developing the setting, time period, and culture in which the story takes place.

For business scenarios, it may require researching industry trends, market dynamics, and potential disruptors.

In educational scenarios, the context and challenges students will face need careful consideration.

Realism is a crucial element in crafting believable scenarios.

To achieve this, scenarios must be rooted in the context and setting they represent.

In storytelling, this means creating consistent and authentic worlds with well-defined rules.

In business scenarios, it involves accurately reflecting market conditions and industry dynamics.

For educational scenarios, realism means presenting challenges and decisions that students may encounter in real-life situations.

Characters play a significant role in scenarios, both in storytelling and educational contexts.

Well-developed characters with distinct motivations, personalities, and backgrounds add depth and authenticity to scenarios.

Readers or participants should be able to relate to these characters, making the scenario more engaging and relatable.

In business scenarios, characters can represent various stakeholders, such as customers, employees, or competitors.

In educational scenarios, characters can embody different perspectives and roles relevant to the learning objectives.

Engagement is a critical factor in the success of scenarios.

Whether in a novel, a business strategy session, or a classroom, scenarios must capture the audience's attention and maintain their interest.

To achieve this, scenarios should include elements of conflict, uncertainty, and decision points that compel readers or participants to become actively involved.

In storytelling, conflict drives the plot forward and keeps readers engaged.

In business scenarios, presenting challenges and dilemmas encourages participants to explore solutions and make decisions.

Educational scenarios should pose questions or problems that require thoughtful responses.

Scenarios often incorporate decision points where characters or participants must choose a course of action.

These decision points are opportunities for readers or participants to engage with the scenario and explore different outcomes based on their choices.

In storytelling, decision points can lead to character development and plot twists.

In business scenarios, they enable participants to test their decision-making skills in a risk-free environment.

In education, decision points encourage critical thinking and problem-solving.

Feedback and consequences are essential components of scenarios.

After characters or participants make decisions, the scenario should provide feedback on the outcomes of those choices.

This feedback helps readers or participants understand the consequences of their actions and learn from their experiences.

In storytelling, feedback can lead to character growth or plot development.

In business scenarios, it informs participants about the impact of their decisions on the organization.

In education, feedback guides students in reflecting on their choices and improving their decision-making skills.

Scenarios can take various forms, depending on their intended use.

In storytelling, scenarios are woven into the narrative, shaping the plot and character arcs.

In business, scenarios are often presented as strategic planning exercises or simulations.

In education, scenarios can be part of case studies, role-playing activities, or interactive simulations.

Regardless of the form, effective scenarios share the common goal of engaging the audience and facilitating learning or decision-making.

Crafting believable scenarios requires a balance between creativity and realism.

Authors, strategists, and educators must create immersive worlds or situations that captivate their audience while staying true to the context and objectives.

Whether used for storytelling, strategic planning, or education, scenarios are a powerful tool for exploring possibilities and developing skills in a dynamic and engaging way.

Chapter 3: Impersonation and Identity Spoofing

Impersonating authority figures is a subject that delves into the intriguing realm of deception and manipulation. This tactic involves pretending to be someone in a position of power or influence to gain trust, compliance, or benefits.

Impersonation can be employed in various contexts, both for malicious purposes and legitimate roles, such as undercover law enforcement operations.

In everyday life, we encounter authority figures regularly, from police officers and government officials to teachers and managers.

These individuals hold positions of power and responsibility, and we generally trust and respect their authority.

Impersonating an authority figure capitalizes on this trust, often with the intention of exploiting it for personal gain or to deceive others.

One common form of authority figure impersonation is the impersonation of law enforcement officers.

Individuals who pose as police officers can intimidate others, gain access to restricted areas, or even commit crimes while using the perceived authority of the uniform.

This impersonation can have serious consequences, as it erodes public trust in law enforcement and can lead to confusion during emergencies.

Impersonating government officials is another deceptive tactic, often seen in scams and fraud.

Individuals may claim to be tax officials, immigration officers, or other government personnel to demand money or personal information from unsuspecting victims.

These scams rely on the belief that government officials have the power to enforce compliance, making people more likely to comply with their demands.

Impersonating teachers or educators is a concern in the context of educational institutions.

In some cases, individuals may pretend to be teachers to access school facilities, interact with students, or even manipulate school records.

These actions can disrupt the learning environment and put students and staff at risk.

On the positive side, impersonating authority figures can serve legitimate purposes.

In undercover law enforcement operations, officers may assume false identities, complete with fake credentials, to infiltrate criminal organizations and gather evidence.

These operations require careful planning and extensive training to maintain the impersonation while upholding the law.

Impersonation tactics can be categorized into two primary types: physical impersonation and digital impersonation.

Physical impersonation involves physically appearing as the authority figure in question.

This can include wearing uniforms, badges, or clothing associated with the role, as well as using body language and speech patterns to mimic the authority figure's behavior.

In contrast, digital impersonation relies on online or electronic means to create the illusion of authority.

For instance, scammers may send emails or messages that appear to come from government agencies or financial institutions, using official logos and language to deceive recipients.

In the digital realm, social engineering attacks can involve impersonating authority figures to manipulate individuals into divulging sensitive information or taking harmful actions.

Impersonating authority figures often requires a deep understanding of the role being mimicked.

Individuals attempting such impersonation must research the authority figure's responsibilities, communication style, and protocols.

In some cases, they may also need to acquire authentic-looking uniforms, badges, or identification.

Additionally, psychological manipulation plays a crucial role in authority figure impersonation.

Perpetrators use psychological tactics to instill fear, compliance, or trust in their targets.

These tactics may include threats of legal consequences, appeals to duty or responsibility, or exploiting emotions like fear, empathy, or respect.

The effectiveness of impersonating authority figures lies in the fact that most people are predisposed to comply with those in positions of power or influence.

This inclination can be traced back to our evolutionary history, where following leaders and authority figures often increased our chances of survival.

Today, this tendency to comply with authority figures is known as the Milgram Effect, a psychological phenomenon observed in Stanley Milgram's famous obedience experiments.

In these experiments, participants were willing to administer what they believed were painful electric shocks to others under the authority's instruction, despite their moral reservations.

Impersonating authority figures leverages this innate tendency, making people more susceptible to manipulation and compliance.

To protect against impersonation tactics, individuals should be vigilant and practice skepticism, especially when faced with unexpected or unusual requests from authority figures.

Verify the identity of the person or organization making the request, and do not hesitate to seek confirmation from official sources.

In the digital age, scrutinize emails, messages, and online interactions for signs of phishing or fraudulent activity.

Educational institutions and organizations should have robust security measures in place to prevent unauthorized access and impersonation.

Training and awareness programs can help employees and students recognize potential threats and take appropriate actions.

In summary, impersonating authority figures is a deceptive tactic that exploits trust and compliance with individuals in positions of power.

While it can be used for legitimate purposes, such as law enforcement operations, it is more commonly associated with scams, fraud, and malicious intent.

Understanding the psychology behind authority figure compliance is essential for recognizing and protecting against impersonation attempts in various contexts, both physical and digital.

Identity theft and spoofing tools represent a significant concern in the world of cybersecurity and digital privacy.

These tools are often used maliciously to impersonate individuals or organizations, leading to various forms of fraud and deception.

Understanding how identity theft and spoofing tools work is crucial for individuals and businesses to protect themselves from cyber threats.

Identity theft occurs when an attacker gains access to personal information, such as a person's name, address, Social Security number, or financial details, and uses it for fraudulent purposes.

Spoofing, on the other hand, involves impersonating someone or something else, often through the manipulation of digital communication.

Identity theft and spoofing tools encompass a wide range of methods and technologies.

One common form of identity theft is phishing, where attackers send deceptive emails or messages to trick individuals into revealing sensitive information.

Phishing emails often appear to come from trusted sources, such as banks, social media platforms, or government agencies, but they are, in fact, fraudulent.

These messages may contain links to fake websites that capture login credentials or prompt users to enter personal information.

To combat phishing, individuals should exercise caution when receiving unsolicited emails and verify the legitimacy of the sender and the message's content.

Another form of identity theft is data breaches, where cybercriminals gain unauthorized access to databases containing personal information.

Once accessed, this data can be sold on the dark web or used to commit various forms of fraud.

To protect against data breaches, organizations should implement robust security measures and regularly update their systems.

Individuals can mitigate the risk of identity theft by using strong, unique passwords and enabling two-factor authentication on their online accounts.

Spoofing tools, on the other hand, focus on impersonation and manipulation of digital communication.

Email spoofing is a prevalent form of spoofing, where attackers alter the sender's email address to appear as if it's coming from a legitimate source.

This tactic is often used in phishing attacks, as it deceives recipients into believing that the email is trustworthy.

To detect email spoofing, individuals should examine the sender's email address and be cautious of unexpected requests for personal information or financial transactions.

Caller ID spoofing is another common technique, allowing attackers to modify the caller ID information displayed on a recipient's phone.

This can be used to impersonate banks, government agencies, or even friends and family, leading to scams or fraud.

To protect against caller ID spoofing, individuals should verify the identity of callers, especially when asked to provide sensitive information or make payments over the phone.

Spoofing tools can also manipulate websites and web traffic.

For example, DNS spoofing involves altering the domain name system (DNS) to redirect users to malicious websites.

This can lead to users unknowingly visiting fraudulent websites that capture sensitive information.

To guard against DNS spoofing, individuals and organizations should use secure DNS servers and employ DNSSEC (DNS Security Extensions) to validate DNS responses.

IP address spoofing is another technique where attackers change the source IP address in network packets to deceive the recipient into believing they are from a trusted source.

This method can be used in distributed denial-of-service (DDoS) attacks to overwhelm a target's servers.

To mitigate the risk of IP address spoofing, network administrators can implement filters and firewalls to block traffic with spoofed IP addresses.

Email header spoofing is a tactic used to manipulate the header information of an email, making it appear as if it came from a different sender.

This can be used to deceive recipients or bypass spam filters.

To identify email header spoofing, individuals can inspect the email's header information for anomalies and inconsistencies.

While identity theft and spoofing tools pose significant risks, there are measures that individuals and organizations can take to protect themselves.

Regularly updating software and operating systems can help patch vulnerabilities that attackers may exploit.

Additionally, using strong, unique passwords and enabling multi-factor authentication can enhance online security.

Education and awareness are also critical components of defense against these threats.

Training individuals to recognize phishing attempts, suspicious emails, and deceptive websites can reduce the likelihood of falling victim to identity theft and spoofing.

Furthermore, organizations should implement robust cybersecurity policies and conduct regular security audits to identify and mitigate potential risks.

In summary, identity theft and spoofing tools are pervasive threats in today's digital landscape.

These tools are used to impersonate individuals and organizations, leading to various forms of deception and fraud.

Understanding the techniques employed by cybercriminals and taking proactive steps to protect personal information and digital communication is essential in safeguarding against these threats.

Chapter 4: Manipulating Human Behavior

Emotional manipulation tactics are techniques used by individuals to control or influence the emotions, thoughts, and behavior of others.

These tactics often involve exploiting emotions such as fear, guilt, or affection to achieve a specific outcome.

Understanding emotional manipulation is crucial for recognizing when it's happening and taking steps to protect oneself.

One common emotional manipulation tactic is guilt-tripping, where an individual uses guilt as a means of control.

This can involve making someone feel responsible for another person's unhappiness or portraying themselves as a victim.

For example, someone might say, "If you loved me, you would do this for me," to make the other person feel guilty and comply with their request.

Another tactic is gaslighting, which involves manipulating someone's perception of reality.

Gaslighters often deny or distort facts, making the victim doubt their own memory or sanity.

They might say things like, "I never said that," or "You're just imagining things," to make the victim question their own recollection of events.

Another emotional manipulation tactic is playing the victim card, where someone portrays themselves as the victim in a situation to gain sympathy or avoid responsibility.

For instance, an individual might say, "I've had such a terrible day; I can't believe you're upset with me now," to deflect blame and elicit sympathy.

Emotional manipulators may also use silent treatment as a tactic.

This involves ignoring or refusing to communicate with someone to make them feel anxious, guilty, or desperate for attention.

They may withdraw affection or communication until the other person complies with their wishes.

Love bombing is another tactic where an individual overwhelms someone with affection and attention in the early stages of a relationship to create dependency and manipulate emotions.

They may shower the person with compliments, gifts, and constant communication to make them feel special and obligated to reciprocate.

Fear tactics involve instilling fear in someone to gain compliance or control.

This can include threats of physical harm, abandonment, or other consequences if the person doesn't do what the manipulator wants.

For instance, an emotional manipulator might say, "If you leave me, you'll never find anyone better," to make the person fear being alone.

Projecting is a tactic where someone accuses others of having the negative qualities or intentions they possess.

They deflect blame by projecting their flaws onto others.

For example, an individual who is dishonest may accuse their partner of being untrustworthy.

Another emotional manipulation tactic is triangulation, which involves involving a third party to create jealousy, competition, or insecurity in a relationship.

This can make one person feel like they have to work harder to gain the manipulator's attention or approval.

Emotional manipulators often use subtle, undermining comments or sarcasm to erode someone's self-esteem and self-worth.

These comments can be masked as jokes or playful teasing but have a detrimental effect over time.

They may say things like, "You're too sensitive," or "Can't you take a joke?"

Another tactic is selective reinforcement, where an emotional manipulator alternates between positive and negative reinforcement to keep the other person off balance.

They may reward good behavior with affection or praise and then withdraw it abruptly when the person doesn't comply with their wishes.

Gaslighting can be a particularly damaging emotional manipulation tactic, as it can lead to the victim questioning their own reality and feeling confused and disoriented.

To protect oneself from emotional manipulation, it's essential to recognize the signs and trust your instincts.

If something doesn't feel right or you notice a pattern of manipulation in a relationship, it's important to establish boundaries and communicate your concerns.

Setting boundaries can help protect your emotional well-being and prevent manipulative tactics from taking hold.

It's also crucial to maintain a support system of friends and loved ones who can provide perspective and emotional support.

Self-esteem and self-worth play a significant role in resisting emotional manipulation.

Building and maintaining a strong sense of self can make it more challenging for manipulators to exploit your emotions.

Learning to assert yourself and communicate your needs and boundaries effectively is essential in dealing with emotional manipulation.

Emotional intelligence, which involves recognizing and managing your own emotions and understanding the emotions of others, can also be a valuable tool in navigating manipulative situations.

In summary, emotional manipulation tactics are used to control or influence the emotions and behavior of others.

These tactics can be subtle and insidious, making it essential to recognize the signs and take steps to protect oneself.

By setting boundaries, maintaining a support system, and developing emotional intelligence, individuals can resist emotional manipulation and maintain healthy relationships based on trust and respect.

Leveraging social dynamics involves understanding and using the complex interactions, behaviors, and norms that occur within social groups.

Social dynamics can be harnessed to achieve various goals, whether in personal relationships, professional settings, or within larger communities.

One fundamental aspect of social dynamics is the concept of social influence, which refers to the ability to change or shape the opinions, attitudes, and behaviors of others.

This can be achieved through various techniques, including persuasion, coercion, or leading by example.

For instance, a charismatic leader may use their influence to inspire their followers to adopt certain beliefs or take specific actions.

Understanding the principles of persuasion is crucial in leveraging social dynamics effectively.

The art of persuasion involves using techniques such as establishing credibility, appealing to emotions, and providing compelling evidence to influence others' decisions.

For example, a salesperson may use persuasive tactics to convince potential customers to purchase a product.

Another essential aspect of social dynamics is group behavior, which examines how individuals behave when they are part of a group.

Group behavior can vary significantly depending on factors such as group size, cohesion, and the presence of a leader.

Leveraging group dynamics can be beneficial in various contexts, from team collaboration in the workplace to organizing social movements.

In a business setting, understanding team dynamics can help leaders create cohesive and productive work environments.

Leaders can encourage collaboration, manage conflicts, and build trust among team members to maximize their effectiveness.

In social movements or advocacy campaigns, organizers can leverage group dynamics to mobilize supporters and create a sense of unity and purpose.

Another element of social dynamics is conformity, which refers to the tendency of individuals to align their beliefs and behaviors with those of a group.

This phenomenon can be observed in everyday situations, from fashion trends to political ideologies.

Leveraging conformity can be advantageous in marketing and advertising, as businesses often seek to create a sense of belonging or the fear of missing out (FOMO) to encourage consumers to follow trends and make purchases.

For example, a fashion brand may promote a particular style as the latest trend to encourage customers to buy their products.

Understanding the principles of conformity and social proof (the idea that people tend to follow the actions of others) can help businesses effectively market their products or services.

Leaders can also use these principles to rally support for their initiatives or causes.

Another aspect of social dynamics is social norms, which are the unwritten rules and expectations that guide behavior within a particular group or society.

Leveraging social norms involves recognizing how they influence people's choices and actions.

For instance, in a workplace with a strong culture of punctuality, employees are more likely to arrive on time for meetings and tasks.

To leverage social norms effectively, individuals and organizations can align their actions and messages with prevailing norms to gain acceptance and cooperation.

However, it's essential to be mindful of the potential ethical implications when leveraging social dynamics.

While understanding and using social dynamics can be advantageous, it's crucial to do so ethically and responsibly, respecting individuals' autonomy and dignity.

Manipulative or coercive tactics that exploit social dynamics for personal gain can have negative consequences and damage trust and relationships.

In summary, leveraging social dynamics involves understanding and using the intricate interactions, behaviors, and norms that occur within social groups.

Social influence, persuasion, group behavior, conformity, and social norms are all essential components of social dynamics that can be harnessed to achieve various goals.

Whether in personal relationships, professional settings, or broader communities, a deep understanding of social dynamics can enhance effectiveness and influence.

Chapter 5: Phishing and Spear Phishing Attacks

Crafting deceptive phishing emails is a technique used by cybercriminals to trick individuals into revealing sensitive information, such as passwords, credit card numbers, or personal data.

Phishing emails often appear legitimate and may imitate reputable organizations, making them difficult to identify as scams.

These emails typically contain malicious links or attachments that, when clicked or opened, can compromise the recipient's security.

Crafting deceptive phishing emails involves several key elements, including the sender's address, subject line, content, and call to action.

One common tactic is to use email addresses that appear to be from trusted sources, such as banks, government agencies, or well-known companies.

Cybercriminals often employ domain spoofing, which involves creating fake email addresses that closely resemble legitimate ones, to deceive recipients.

For example, they might use "support@paypai.com" instead of "support@paypal.com" to trick users into believing the email is from PayPal.

The subject line of a phishing email is critical in capturing the recipient's attention and generating a sense of urgency or curiosity.

Crafters of deceptive emails often use subject lines like "Account Suspension," "Urgent Action Required," or "Security Alert" to elicit a response.

These subject lines create a sense of urgency, prompting recipients to open the email immediately.

The content of phishing emails typically includes text and graphics designed to mimic official correspondence.

Cybercriminals may use logos, fonts, and formatting that closely resemble those of the targeted organization to create a convincing appearance.

The body of the email often contains a message that preys on the recipient's emotions, such as fear, curiosity, or greed.

For example, a phishing email may claim that the recipient's account has been compromised and that urgent action is needed to prevent unauthorized access.

To further deceive recipients, the email may include a call to action, such as clicking on a link or downloading an attachment to verify account information or resolve the issue.

Phishing emails may also employ psychological tactics, such as creating a sense of fear or urgency.

For instance, they may threaten account suspension, legal action, or financial loss if the recipient does not comply with the instructions.

Crafters of deceptive phishing emails often use social engineering techniques to manipulate recipients into taking the desired actions.

These techniques may include appealing to the recipient's sense of altruism, curiosity, or trust.

For example, an email may claim that a donation is needed to help a sick child or that a long-lost relative has left them a substantial inheritance.

To make the email appear more authentic, phishing emails may include seemingly legitimate links to websites that imitate the organization they are impersonating.

These links may redirect to fake login pages where recipients are prompted to enter their credentials, which are then captured by the cybercriminals.

Crafting deceptive phishing emails requires careful attention to detail and a deep understanding of human psychology.

Cybercriminals often conduct extensive research on their targets to create highly personalized and convincing messages.

They may gather information from social media profiles, online forums, or data breaches to make their emails appear more credible.

To protect against deceptive phishing emails, individuals should exercise caution and follow best practices for email security.

These practices include verifying the sender's email address, avoiding clicking on suspicious links or downloading attachments from unknown sources, and using strong, unique passwords for online accounts.

In addition, email filters and antivirus software can help detect and block phishing emails.

Organizations should also educate their employees about the risks of phishing attacks and provide training on how to recognize and report suspicious emails.

In summary, crafting deceptive phishing emails is a technique used by cybercriminals to trick individuals into revealing sensitive information.

These emails often appear legitimate and employ various tactics to manipulate recipients into taking the desired actions.

To protect against phishing attacks, individuals and organizations should be vigilant and follow best practices for email security.

Targeted spear phishing techniques represent an advanced form of cyberattack that focuses on specific individuals or organizations.

These attacks are highly personalized and tailored to the preferences, interests, and behaviors of the intended victims.

Unlike generic phishing campaigns that cast a wide net in the hope of catching unsuspecting individuals, spear phishing is precise and strategic.

To execute successful targeted spear phishing attacks, cybercriminals invest time and effort into researching their victims.

They gather information from various sources, including social media, online forums, company websites, and public records.

By understanding the victim's personal and professional life, attackers can craft convincing and contextually relevant phishing emails.

One common approach in spear phishing is impersonating a trusted entity or individual.

Attackers often pose as colleagues, supervisors, or trusted contacts to establish credibility and trust with the victim.

For example, an attacker may impersonate the victim's boss and send an urgent email requesting sensitive financial information.

The email may be carefully crafted to mimic the boss's writing style and use terminology consistent with the organization's communication norms.

To make their attacks even more convincing, cybercriminals sometimes compromise the email accounts of trusted individuals.

Once they gain access to a trusted email account, attackers can send fraudulent messages from within the organization's own communication platform.

This level of sophistication can significantly increase the chances of success.

Another technique in targeted spear phishing is pretexting, where attackers create a fabricated scenario to manipulate the victim into taking a specific action.

For instance, an attacker may send an email posing as the IT department, claiming there's been a security breach and asking the victim to reset their password by clicking on a link.

The pretext creates a sense of urgency and concern, prompting the victim to act quickly without questioning the email's legitimacy.

Attackers may also exploit current events or trends to make their spear phishing emails more convincing.

For example, during the COVID-19 pandemic, there was a surge in phishing emails related to the virus, capitalizing on people's fears and uncertainties.

These emails promised information about the pandemic, such as safety measures or vaccine availability, to lure victims into clicking on malicious links.

Another tactic used in spear phishing is the use of highly targeted malware attachments or links.

Attackers may attach malware-laden documents or embed malicious links within emails to compromise the victim's device or network.

These attachments often masquerade as legitimate files, such as invoices, reports, or presentations.

Once opened, they can infect the victim's system with malware that steals sensitive data or provides remote access to the attacker.

Spear phishing attacks may also involve exploiting the victim's emotions and psychological vulnerabilities.

For example, an attacker may craft an email that plays on the victim's fear of public embarrassment or legal consequences.

The email might threaten to expose sensitive information or engage in blackmail unless the victim complies with the attacker's demands.

Furthermore, attackers may use social engineering tactics to manipulate victims into disclosing sensitive information.

They may engage in prolonged email exchanges, gaining the victim's trust over time before requesting confidential data.

Alternatively, attackers may impersonate a colleague or friend and engage in casual conversations to gather information gradually.

Defending against targeted spear phishing techniques requires a multi-faceted approach.

First, organizations should invest in robust cybersecurity measures, including email filtering, endpoint protection, and network monitoring.

User education and awareness training are also crucial, as employees are often the first line of defense against spear phishing attacks.

Training should include recognizing common phishing red flags, verifying the authenticity of emails, and reporting suspicious messages promptly.

Additionally, organizations should implement strong access controls and authentication methods to limit the potential impact of successful spear phishing attacks.

Regularly updating software and patching vulnerabilities can also help mitigate the risk of malware infections through email attachments or links.

Individuals should exercise caution when receiving unsolicited emails, especially those that create a sense of urgency or contain unexpected attachments or links.

Verifying the sender's identity through a separate communication channel can help confirm the legitimacy of the email.

In summary, targeted spear phishing techniques represent a highly sophisticated form of cyberattack that relies on precision, personalization, and deception.

Attackers invest time in researching their victims, crafting convincing emails, and exploiting psychological vulnerabilities to achieve their objectives.

Defending against these attacks requires a combination of robust cybersecurity measures, user education, and vigilant awareness.

Chapter 6: Physical Security Exploits

Tailgating and piggybacking are physical security breaches that occur when an unauthorized person gains access to a secure area by closely following an authorized individual.

These tactics exploit the natural courtesy of people who hold the door open for others, allowing unauthorized individuals to enter restricted spaces.

Tailgating occurs when a person without proper credentials or permission follows an authorized person through a secure access point, such as a locked door or a turnstile.

Piggybacking is a similar technique, but it involves a more passive approach, where the unauthorized person doesn't actively follow but rather relies on someone else's access to gain entry.

These social engineering tactics can be used to infiltrate high-security areas, such as office buildings, data centers, or research facilities.

Tailgating and piggybacking are particularly effective in environments where employees are accustomed to holding the door for colleagues or visitors.

Attackers often take advantage of this human tendency to appear inconspicuous and gain access to sensitive areas without raising suspicion.

In many cases, the unauthorized person may dress and behave in a way that makes them seem like a legitimate employee or visitor.

They might carry a briefcase, wear a uniform, or act confidently to blend in with the crowd.

In some instances, tailgating and piggybacking can be used as part of a larger plan to steal sensitive information or assets from an organization.

For example, an attacker could enter a secure office space, steal confidential documents, or plant surveillance devices to gather valuable intelligence.

These tactics can also be employed by malicious insiders seeking to exploit their access for nefarious purposes.

To prevent tailgating and piggybacking, organizations should implement strict access control measures, such as electronic card readers, biometric authentication, or security personnel stationed at entrances.

These measures help ensure that only authorized individuals can gain entry to secure areas.

Employees should be trained to recognize the importance of not allowing others to tailgate or piggyback and to report any suspicious behavior immediately.

Additionally, security policies should emphasize the importance of verifying the identity of visitors and challenging anyone who attempts to gain access without proper authorization.

Visitor badges, escorting protocols, and clearly defined access procedures can all contribute to a more secure environment.

Security awareness programs can play a vital role in educating employees about the risks of tailgating and piggybacking.

Employees should be made aware of the potential consequences of these security breaches and be encouraged to be vigilant and proactive in maintaining physical security.

To further enhance security, organizations may use security cameras to monitor access points and review footage to identify any suspicious incidents.

Physical security audits can help identify vulnerabilities and weaknesses in access control systems and procedures.

Tailgating and piggybacking can also be mitigated by implementing mantrap systems, which consist of an enclosed area with two interlocking doors.

Access is granted only when an individual is authenticated and authorized, preventing unauthorized entry even if an authorized person holds the door open.

In summary, tailgating and piggybacking are social engineering tactics that exploit human courtesy to gain unauthorized access to secure areas.

These tactics can pose significant security risks to organizations, as they allow individuals with malicious intent to enter restricted spaces.

Preventing tailgating and piggybacking requires a combination of access control measures, employee training, and security awareness programs to maintain physical security.

Lock picking and bypass techniques are skills and methods used to gain unauthorized access to locked spaces or objects.

These techniques have been around for centuries and are often associated with locksmiths and security professionals who use them for legitimate purposes.

However, they can also be exploited by criminals and malicious actors to break into homes, buildings, or secure containers.

Lock picking involves manipulating the internal components of a lock to open it without using the correct key.

The primary tools for lock picking include lock picks, tension wrenches, and sometimes other specialized tools, depending on the type of lock being targeted.

Lock picks come in various shapes and sizes, each designed for specific lock configurations and mechanisms.

The tension wrench is used to apply rotational force to the lock's core, allowing the lock picker to set the individual pins or components inside.

The goal is to align all the pins or components at the shear line, enabling the core to rotate and unlock the door or device.

Lock picking requires skill, precision, and knowledge of lock mechanisms, making it a method often used by hobbyists and those in the locksmith profession.

Bypass techniques, on the other hand, involve exploiting weaknesses or vulnerabilities in the locking system to open it without picking the lock directly.

One common bypass technique is known as "bumping," which involves using a specially crafted bump key to rapidly strike the key pins inside the lock.

This action can cause the pins to jump and align momentarily at the shear line, allowing the lock to be turned and opened.

Bumping is a relatively quick method and can be effective on many types of pin tumbler locks.

Another bypass technique is called "impressioning," where an attacker creates a duplicate key by making an impression of the lock's keyway using a blank key.

By inserting and manipulating the blank key repeatedly, marks are left on the key that correspond to the position of the pins inside the lock.

These marks are then used to file the blank key until it can successfully open the lock.

Impressioning requires patience and practice but can be a highly effective method.

Lock bypass methods also extend to electronic locks, where attackers may exploit vulnerabilities in the electronic control systems to gain unauthorized access.

This can involve techniques such as exploiting weak or default passwords, using electronic "bypass tools," or taking advantage of software vulnerabilities.

While lock picking and bypass techniques can be used for legitimate purposes, such as locksmithing or lock maintenance, they can also be employed for criminal activities, including burglary and theft.

To protect against these techniques, individuals and organizations should employ robust physical security measures.

This includes using high-quality locks and deadbolts, as well as considering electronic access control systems that offer greater security.

Security professionals should conduct regular security audits to identify vulnerabilities in physical access control systems and address them promptly.

In addition, educating employees and residents about the importance of security and reporting any suspicious activity can help deter lock picking and bypass attempts. For individuals concerned about home security, reinforcing door frames, installing security bars or chains, and using additional security devices can provide added protection.

In summary, lock picking and bypass techniques are methods used to gain unauthorized access to locked spaces or objects by manipulating lock mechanisms or exploiting vulnerabilities.

While these techniques have legitimate uses, they can also be employed for criminal activities.

To protect against lock picking and bypass attempts, individuals and organizations should implement strong physical security measures and conduct regular security assessments.

Chapter 7: Psychological Manipulation in Social Engineering

Influence techniques and mind games are strategies and tactics used to manipulate and persuade individuals to think, feel, or act in a certain way.

These techniques are often employed in various aspects of life, from marketing and advertising to politics and personal relationships.

Understanding how influence techniques work can help individuals make informed decisions and resist undue persuasion.

One common influence technique is the use of reciprocity, which involves giving something to someone in the hope that they will feel obliged to return the favor.

For example, a salesperson might offer a free sample of a product, creating a sense of indebtedness in the recipient.

Reciprocity taps into the human instinct to repay kindness or favors and can be a powerful tool in influencing behavior.

Another technique is social proof, where people tend to follow the actions or choices of others, especially in uncertain or ambiguous situations.

When individuals see others engaging in a particular behavior or making a specific choice, they are more likely to do the same.

This principle is often used in marketing through testimonials, user reviews, and endorsements to create a sense of consensus and trust.

Scarcity is another effective influence technique, where the perceived limited availability of a product or opportunity can increase its desirability.

Individuals are more inclined to act quickly or make a purchase if they believe that what is being offered is scarce or in high demand.

Scarcity leverages the fear of missing out and can create a sense of urgency.

Consistency is a cognitive bias that drives individuals to align their actions with their previously stated beliefs or commitments.

When people make a public commitment or express their views, they tend to stick with them to maintain consistency in their self-image.

This influence technique is often used in marketing by getting individuals to make small commitments or statements that lead them toward larger actions.

Authority is a technique that relies on the perception of credibility and expertise.

People are more likely to follow the guidance or recommendations of individuals they perceive as authoritative figures or experts in a particular field.

This principle is often employed by professionals, influencers, and celebrities to promote products or ideas.

Liking is an influence technique that involves building rapport and a sense of connection with others.

People are more likely to be influenced by those they like, admire, or feel a personal connection with.

This is why many marketing campaigns focus on building positive relationships and associations with their target audience.

Fear and scarcity are often used in advertising and marketing to create a sense of urgency and drive action.

For example, limited-time offers, countdowns, and statements like "only a few left" can trigger fear of missing out and prompt individuals to make a purchase.

Influence techniques and mind games can also be used in personal relationships and social interactions.

People may employ these tactics to persuade others to agree with their viewpoints, make concessions, or change their behavior.

Recognizing when influence techniques are being used can help individuals make more informed decisions and avoid being manipulated.

Critical thinking and skepticism are valuable skills in navigating a world filled with persuasive messages and influence attempts.

It's important to evaluate information and claims critically, consider alternative perspectives, and make decisions based on one's own values and priorities.

In summary, influence techniques and mind games are powerful tools used to manipulate and persuade individuals in various contexts.

Understanding how these techniques work can help individuals make informed decisions and resist undue influence.

By being aware of the principles behind these tactics, individuals can navigate a world filled with persuasive messages and make choices that align with their values and preferences.

Exploiting emotional triggers is a common technique used in various forms of persuasion and manipulation. Understanding how emotions influence decision-making can shed light on how individuals and organizations can use emotional triggers to achieve their goals.

Emotions play a significant role in the choices people make, often guiding their decisions more than rational thinking.

Positive emotions like happiness, excitement, and love can drive individuals to engage in certain behaviors or make specific choices.

Conversely, negative emotions such as fear, anger, and sadness can also influence decision-making but in different ways.

For instance, fear can lead people to take action to avoid a perceived threat, while anger can motivate them to confront or challenge a perceived injustice.

Marketers and advertisers frequently employ emotional triggers in their campaigns to create a connection between a product or service and a specific emotion.

For example, an advertisement for a luxury car may aim to evoke feelings of status, prestige, and admiration.

This emotional trigger can lead consumers to associate the car with a sense of achievement and success, driving them to make a purchase.

Similarly, public service announcements often use emotional triggers to encourage behavior change.

Anti-smoking campaigns, for instance, may employ fear-based messaging to provoke feelings of dread about the health risks associated with smoking.

This emotional trigger can motivate individuals to quit smoking or never start in the first place.

In the realm of politics, emotional triggers are frequently used to sway public opinion and garner support.

Political speeches and campaigns often tap into emotions like hope, fear, and anger to rally voters and drive them to take action.

For instance, a politician may use rhetoric that stirs hope for a brighter future, prompting people to vote for change.

On the other hand, they may also use fear to highlight the potential consequences of not voting for their candidate.

In interpersonal relationships, understanding and using emotional triggers can have both positive and negative consequences.

Individuals may employ emotional triggers to strengthen bonds, mend conflicts, or manipulate others.

For instance, expressing empathy and understanding when someone is feeling sad can strengthen a friendship or relationship.

On the flip side, using guilt as an emotional trigger can manipulate someone into doing something they may not want to do.

It's essential to recognize the ethical implications of exploiting emotional triggers, as it can lead to harm and damage trust.

In the context of social engineering and cyberattacks, exploiting emotional triggers is a common tactic.

Phishing emails, for example, often use emotional triggers to deceive recipients into taking action, such as clicking on malicious links or providing sensitive information.

These emails may create a sense of urgency, fear, or curiosity to prompt individuals to react without thinking critically.

Emotional manipulation in cyberattacks can also involve impersonating trusted entities, like a colleague or a bank, to deceive victims into complying with requests.

Understanding the psychology of emotional triggers is crucial for individuals to protect themselves against such tactics.

Recognizing the signs of emotional manipulation can help people make informed decisions and avoid falling victim to scams and cyberattacks.

Emotional intelligence, which involves recognizing and managing one's own emotions as well as understanding the emotions of others, can be a valuable skill in navigating situations where emotional triggers are at play.

In personal relationships, empathy, active listening, and open communication can promote healthy emotional connections and minimize the potential for manipulation.

In summary, exploiting emotional triggers is a pervasive and powerful technique used in various aspects of life, from marketing and politics to interpersonal relationships and cyberattacks.

Emotions play a significant role in decision-making, and understanding how they can be influenced is essential for individuals and organizations alike.

Recognizing the ethical implications of using emotional triggers is crucial to maintaining trust and healthy relationships.

Individuals can protect themselves by developing emotional intelligence and being vigilant against emotional manipulation in all aspects of life.

Chapter 8: Advanced Social Engineering Techniques

Using the Social Engineering Toolkit (SET) effectively is a crucial skill for red team professionals and ethical hackers.

SET is a versatile and powerful tool that allows individuals to simulate social engineering attacks and assess the security of systems and organizations.

Before diving into SET usage, it's essential to understand its primary purpose and how it fits into the larger field of red teaming and ethical hacking.

SET is designed to automate and simplify the process of crafting and executing social engineering attacks.

It provides a range of pre-built attack vectors and templates that make it easier for security professionals to test and assess an organization's security posture.

One of the key advantages of using SET is its ability to generate realistic and convincing phishing campaigns.

Phishing remains one of the most common and successful attack vectors, and organizations need to be vigilant in defending against it.

With SET, users can create phishing emails, websites, and payloads that closely mimic legitimate communications and websites.

This enables them to assess an organization's susceptibility to phishing attacks and identify areas for improvement.

To use SET effectively, one must first install and configure the toolkit on their system.

SET is open-source software and can be downloaded and installed on various operating systems, including Linux and Windows.

Once SET is installed, users can launch it and access its menu-driven interface, which simplifies the process of creating and launching attacks.

SET provides a range of attack vectors, including spear-phishing, credential harvesting, and malicious file delivery.

Each attack vector is accompanied by detailed instructions and options that allow users to customize their attacks to suit their specific goals and scenarios.

For example, the credential harvesting attack vector allows users to set up fake login pages for popular services like Gmail or Facebook.

Users can then send phishing emails or messages that direct targets to these fake login pages, where their credentials are captured.

Another powerful feature of SET is its ability to create malicious payloads that can be delivered to targets.

These payloads can include various types of malware or backdoors that, when executed, provide attackers with access to the target's system.

Payloads generated by SET are often tailored to bypass antivirus and security solutions, making them more effective.

To use SET's payload generation capabilities, users can select the payload they want to create, customize it with options such as obfuscation and encoding, and then deliver it to the target.

The toolkit also supports the creation of weaponized documents, such as malicious PDFs or Word documents, which can be used to exploit vulnerabilities in document viewers and editors.

In addition to creating and delivering attacks, SET includes features for tracking and collecting data on the success of these attacks.

Users can set up email tracking, web tracking, and credential capture to monitor the interactions of their targets.

This data can provide valuable insights into the effectiveness of an attack and help red team professionals refine their tactics.

While SET is a valuable tool for red teaming and ethical hacking, it's essential to emphasize that its usage should always be ethical and legal.

It should only be employed for legitimate security testing and assessment purposes with proper authorization.

Unauthorized and malicious use of SET can have serious legal and ethical consequences.

Furthermore, SET should be used responsibly to avoid causing harm to individuals or organizations.

As with any powerful tool, it's crucial for users to be knowledgeable about the laws and regulations governing their activities and to always obtain proper permissions and consents.

In summary, the Social Engineering Toolkit (SET) is a valuable resource for red team professionals and ethical hackers.

It simplifies the process of crafting and executing social engineering attacks, allowing security experts to assess an organization's security posture and identify vulnerabilities.

SET offers a range of attack vectors, payload generation capabilities, and tracking features to support these efforts.

However, its usage should always be ethical, legal, and responsible, with proper authorization and consent to avoid potential harm or legal repercussions.

Open-source intelligence (OSINT) and target profiling are critical components of red team operations and ethical hacking.

OSINT involves collecting and analyzing information from publicly available sources to gather insights about a target, which can include individuals, organizations, or systems.

The goal of OSINT is to gather data that can be used to understand the target's vulnerabilities, weaknesses, and potential attack vectors.

Target profiling, on the other hand, is the process of creating a detailed profile of the target based on the information gathered through OSINT.

This profile can include information such as the target's personnel, technologies in use, network architecture, and potential security gaps.

To conduct effective OSINT, red team professionals and ethical hackers rely on a variety of tools and techniques.

These can include search engines, social media platforms, public records, online forums, and specialized OSINT tools.

Search engines like Google are valuable resources for finding publicly available information about a target.

By using advanced search operators and filters, OSINT analysts can narrow down their search results to focus on specific types of data.

Social media platforms are also rich sources of information, providing insights into an individual's personal life, interests, and connections.

Red team professionals can use this information to craft convincing social engineering attacks or spear-phishing campaigns.

Public records, such as property records, business registrations, and court documents, can reveal important details about an organization or individual.

Online forums and communities may provide discussions and insights related to a target's technologies, vulnerabilities, and security practices.

Specialized OSINT tools, like Maltego and Shodan, can automate the process of gathering and analyzing data from various sources.

When conducting OSINT, it's crucial to respect ethical boundaries and legal restrictions.

Red team professionals must ensure that they are not engaging in activities that violate privacy or break the law.

Obtaining information through legal and ethical means is essential to maintaining the integrity of the assessment.

Once OSINT data is collected, the next step is target profiling.

This involves organizing and analyzing the information to create a comprehensive profile of the target.

Target profiling typically includes identifying key personnel within an organization, such as executives or system administrators.

It also involves mapping out the organization's network architecture and identifying potential entry points and vulnerabilities.

By analyzing the information gathered during OSINT, red team professionals can identify potential weaknesses and areas for exploitation.

For example, they may discover that an organization's employees frequently share sensitive information on social media platforms.

This information can be used to craft a spear-phishing campaign targeting those employees.

Or, they may find that a particular software version is widely used within an organization and has known vulnerabilities.

In this case, the red team may focus on exploiting those vulnerabilities during their assessment.

Effective target profiling can help red team professionals prioritize their efforts and tailor their attack strategies to the specific weaknesses of the target.

It allows them to craft more convincing and targeted attacks, increasing the likelihood of success.

It's important to note that OSINT and target profiling are ongoing processes.

As new information becomes available and the target's environment evolves, red team professionals must continuously update their assessments.

This ensures that their attack strategies remain relevant and effective.

In addition to their technical skills, red team professionals and ethical hackers must possess strong analytical and research abilities.

They must be adept at sifting through vast amounts of data to identify relevant and actionable information.

They must also be skilled at connecting the dots between seemingly unrelated pieces of information to uncover hidden vulnerabilities.

Furthermore, they should be aware of potential biases in their analysis and strive to maintain objectivity.

In summary, OSINT and target profiling are fundamental components of red team operations and ethical hacking.

They involve gathering and analyzing publicly available information to create detailed profiles of targets.

These profiles inform attack strategies and help red team professionals identify vulnerabilities and weaknesses.

To be effective in OSINT and target profiling, individuals must have strong research and analytical skills while also adhering to ethical and legal boundaries.

Chapter 9: Social Engineering in Red Team Operations

Integrating social engineering with red teaming is a sophisticated approach that enhances the effectiveness of security assessments.

Social engineering is the practice of manipulating individuals into divulging confidential information or taking specific actions that benefit the attacker.

In red teaming, it involves using psychological tactics to exploit human weaknesses and gain unauthorized access to systems or facilities.

By combining social engineering with traditional red teaming techniques, security professionals can assess an organization's overall security posture more comprehensively.

Social engineering attacks can take various forms, such as phishing emails, pretexting, tailgating, and impersonation.

These attacks often rely on psychological manipulation and the exploitation of cognitive biases to deceive targets.

Phishing emails, for example, may use deceptive tactics to trick recipients into clicking on malicious links or downloading malware.

Pretexting involves creating a fabricated scenario to gain a target's trust and access to sensitive information.

Tailgating and impersonation tactics rely on manipulating physical security measures and human trust to gain unauthorized entry to secure locations.

The integration of social engineering into red teaming begins with thorough planning and reconnaissance.

Red team professionals research the target organization to identify potential weaknesses and gather information that can be leveraged in social engineering attacks.

This research includes identifying key personnel, understanding the organizational culture, and assessing security awareness levels.

With this information in hand, red teamers can craft convincing social engineering scenarios that align with the target's environment.

A successful integration of social engineering with red teaming requires a multi-pronged approach that encompasses both technical and human-focused tactics.

Phishing campaigns, for instance, may be used to deliver malware or gain initial access to a network.

These campaigns often involve crafting persuasive emails that mimic legitimate communication from trusted sources.

The goal is to exploit recipients' trust and curiosity, leading them to take actions that compromise security.

Once initial access is achieved, red team professionals can pivot to technical attacks, leveraging the compromised system as a foothold to further infiltrate the network.

Social engineering can also be used to manipulate employees or gain physical access to facilities.

Pretexting scenarios can be developed to convince employees to disclose sensitive information, such as login credentials or proprietary data.

Tailgating and impersonation tactics can be employed to breach physical security measures, bypass access controls, and enter restricted areas.

One of the key benefits of integrating social engineering with red teaming is the realistic assessment it provides.

By emulating real-world attack scenarios, organizations can better understand their vulnerabilities and the potential impact of social engineering attacks.

This allows them to fine-tune their security policies, training programs, and incident response procedures.

However, it's essential to conduct social engineering assessments responsibly and ethically, adhering to legal and ethical boundaries.

It's important to obtain proper authorization from the target organization and ensure that assessments do not cause harm or violate privacy.

In addition, red team professionals must always prioritize safety and maintain a clear line of communication with the target organization to avoid any misunderstandings.

Furthermore, organizations should view social engineering assessments as an opportunity for education and improvement.

Identifying weaknesses in human behavior and security awareness can lead to more effective training programs and awareness campaigns.

These efforts can empower employees to recognize and resist social engineering attacks, reducing the organization's overall risk.

In summary, integrating social engineering with red teaming is a valuable approach for assessing an organization's security posture comprehensively.

It involves leveraging psychological manipulation and cognitive biases to exploit human weaknesses and gain access to systems or facilities.

When conducted responsibly and ethically, social engineering assessments can provide valuable insights into an organization's vulnerabilities and help enhance its security defenses.

By combining technical and human-focused tactics, red team professionals can emulate real-world attack scenarios and assist organizations in improving their security measures and employee awareness.

Coordinated attack scenarios represent a complex and multifaceted approach to security assessments and red teaming exercises. In these scenarios, multiple attack vectors and techniques are orchestrated and executed simultaneously to mimic a coordinated cyberattack.

The primary objective of coordinated attack scenarios is to evaluate an organization's ability to detect, respond to, and mitigate advanced threats that involve a combination of tactics, techniques, and procedures. These scenarios require meticulous planning, coordination, and execution to accurately replicate the sophistication of real-world cyberattacks.

One common element in coordinated attack scenarios is the use of a red team, which is a group of skilled security professionals tasked with simulating adversarial threats. Red team members leverage their expertise in various domains, such as penetration testing, social engineering, malware analysis, and vulnerability assessment, to devise a comprehensive attack strategy.

Coordinated attack scenarios encompass a wide range of cybersecurity threats and techniques, including but not limited to:

Advanced Persistent Threats (APTs): APTs are stealthy and long-term cyberattacks conducted by well-funded and organized threat actors. Coordinated attack scenarios may include APT-like tactics to assess an organization's ability to detect and respond to persistent threats.

Spear Phishing: Coordinated attacks often involve spear phishing campaigns, which target specific individuals within an organization using personalized and convincing lures to compromise their systems or credentials.

Malware Deployment: Red teams may deploy various types of malware, such as ransomware or remote access trojans, to assess an organization's capability to detect and contain malicious software.

Insider Threat Simulation: Coordinated scenarios can simulate insider threats, where red team members, either posing as employees or collaborating with insiders, attempt to exfiltrate sensitive data or compromise systems from within.

Physical Security Breaches: In some cases, coordinated attack scenarios may extend beyond digital threats to include physical security breaches. This can involve tactics like unauthorized entry, social engineering to gain physical access, or theft of physical assets.

Covert Data Exfiltration: Coordinated attacks may test an organization's ability to prevent unauthorized data exfiltration, with red team members attempting to exfiltrate sensitive information without detection.

Lateral Movement: To mimic real-world attacks, red team members may move laterally within an organization's network, attempting to escalate privileges and gain access to critical systems.

Evasion Techniques: Coordinated attack scenarios often incorporate evasion techniques to bypass security controls, such as intrusion detection systems and firewalls, to maintain persistent access.

Denial of Service (DoS) Attacks: These scenarios may involve DoS attacks to assess an organization's resilience and response to service interruptions.

Cloud Security Assessment: As organizations increasingly adopt cloud services, coordinated scenarios may include assessments of cloud security controls, emphasizing potential weaknesses and misconfigurations.

Throughout coordinated attack scenarios, detailed logs and documentation are maintained to track the red team's actions and the organization's responses. This documentation is invaluable for post-assessment analysis and remediation efforts.

By conducting coordinated attack scenarios, organizations gain valuable insights into their security posture, incident response capabilities, and the effectiveness of their security controls. These assessments can uncover vulnerabilities that might otherwise remain undetected in isolated assessments and help organizations proactively improve their defenses against multifaceted threats.

It is essential to approach coordinated attack scenarios with a comprehensive and well-defined scope, ensuring that they align with the organization's risk tolerance and security objectives. Additionally, these scenarios should be conducted with full transparency and collaboration between the red team and the organization's security and IT teams to facilitate knowledge transfer and foster a culture of continuous improvement in cybersecurity defenses.

In summary, coordinated attack scenarios represent a sophisticated approach to security assessments, involving multiple attack vectors and techniques to evaluate an organization's readiness to defend against advanced threats. These scenarios encompass a wide range of cybersecurity threats, including APTs, spear phishing, malware deployment, insider threats, and physical security breaches. Conducting coordinated attack scenarios helps organizations identify vulnerabilities, improve incident response capabilities, and enhance their overall security posture.

Chapter 10: Mitigating Social Engineering Threats

Employee training and awareness programs play a pivotal role in strengthening an organization's cybersecurity defenses. In today's digital landscape, where cyber threats are constantly evolving, employees are often the first line of defense against malicious actors. These programs are designed to educate and empower employees to recognize, respond to, and mitigate security risks effectively.

At the heart of these programs is the recognition that employees can be both the strongest and weakest links in an organization's security posture. While well-trained employees can identify and thwart phishing attempts, malware infections, and social engineering tactics, those lacking awareness may unwittingly become conduits for cyberattacks.

The foundation of employee training and awareness programs lies in education. Employees need to understand the significance of cybersecurity and the potential consequences of security breaches, both for the organization and themselves. This awareness encourages a sense of shared responsibility for safeguarding sensitive data and digital assets.

Effective employee training programs should cover a range of topics, including:

Phishing Awareness: Phishing is a prevalent cyber threat, and employees must learn to recognize suspicious emails, links, and attachments. Training programs often include simulated phishing campaigns to test employees' ability to discern legitimate from malicious communications.

Password Security: Employees should be educated on the importance of strong, unique passwords and encouraged to use password managers to enhance security. They must also understand the risks associated with password sharing and reuse.

Social Engineering: Training should address various social engineering tactics, such as pretexting, baiting, and tailgating. Employees should be able to identify attempts to manipulate or deceive them.

Malware Awareness: Employees need to recognize the signs of malware infections and understand the consequences of downloading and executing suspicious files or programs.

Data Protection: Employees must be aware of the organization's data protection policies, including the handling of sensitive information, secure file sharing, and proper data disposal.

Mobile Device Security: In today's mobile-driven world, it's essential to educate employees about the security risks associated with mobile devices and the importance of keeping them up-to-date and protected.

Remote Work Security: With the rise of remote work, employees need guidance on securing their home networks, using virtual private networks (VPNs), and adhering to security protocols while working outside the office.

Incident Reporting: Training programs should emphasize the importance of reporting security incidents promptly and provide clear procedures for reporting suspicious activity.

Security Policies and Procedures: Employees should be familiar with the organization's security policies, including acceptable use policies, password policies, and incident response plans.

Security Culture: Beyond specific knowledge, training programs aim to foster a cybersecurity-conscious culture within the organization, where security becomes an integral part of daily operations.

To be effective, these programs should be ongoing and adapted to address emerging threats and technologies. Security awareness is not a one-time event but an ongoing process that evolves alongside the threat landscape.

Engagement is a critical factor in the success of employee training and awareness programs. Dry, mandatory training sessions are unlikely to be as effective as interactive, engaging experiences. Gamification, quizzes, and real-world scenarios can make training more enjoyable and memorable.

Moreover, training should be tailored to different roles within the organization. IT staff may require more technical training, while non-technical employees benefit from broader awareness programs. Regular testing and assessments can help identify areas where additional training is needed.

Employee training and awareness programs are not just about mitigating risks; they also contribute to a culture of security within the organization. When employees understand the role they play in safeguarding the organization's assets and reputation, they become active participants in the ongoing battle against cyber threats. In this way, training and awareness programs become an investment in both cybersecurity and the overall well-being of the organization.

Implementing strong access controls is a fundamental aspect of ensuring the security and integrity of an organization's digital assets. In today's interconnected and data-driven world, protecting sensitive information from unauthorized access is paramount. Access controls are the mechanisms and policies that determine who can access what resources within an organization's network, systems, and applications.

The need for robust access controls arises from several factors. First and foremost is the ever-present threat of unauthorized access. Malicious actors constantly seek ways to infiltrate systems, steal data, or disrupt operations. Implementing strong access controls is the first line of defense against such threats.

Another factor driving the importance of access controls is compliance with regulations and standards. Many industries are subject to strict data protection regulations, such as the General Data Protection Regulation (GDPR) in Europe or the Health Insurance Portability and Accountability Act (HIPAA) in the healthcare sector. Compliance with these regulations often requires organizations to implement stringent access controls to safeguard sensitive data.

Effective access controls involve a combination of technical measures and well-defined policies and procedures. Here are key components and considerations in implementing strong access controls:

User Authentication: User authentication is the process of verifying the identity of individuals or entities trying to access a system or resource. Passwords, biometrics, and multi-factor authentication (MFA) are common authentication methods.

Authorization: Authorization determines what actions or resources authenticated users are allowed to access. Role-based access control (RBAC) is a common approach, where permissions are assigned based on a user's role within the organization.

Least Privilege: The principle of least privilege (POLP) ensures that users are granted only the minimum level of access necessary to perform their job functions. This reduces the risk of accidental or intentional misuse of privileges.

Access Policies: Access control policies define who can access specific resources and what actions they can perform. These policies should align with the organization's security and business requirements.

Access Reviews: Regularly reviewing and updating access rights is essential to maintain security. Employees' roles may change, and access requirements can evolve over time.

Monitoring and Logging: Implementing monitoring and logging mechanisms allows organizations to track user activities and detect suspicious or unauthorized access attempts. Security Information and Event Management (SIEM) systems can assist in this aspect.

Encryption: Data encryption ensures that even if unauthorized access occurs, the data remains protected. Implementing encryption for data at rest and in transit is a critical security measure.

Auditing and Reporting: Organizations should have the ability to generate access-related reports and audit trails to demonstrate compliance and investigate security incidents.

Access Control for Third Parties: When granting access to third parties, such as vendors or partners, organizations should implement controls to limit their access and monitor their activities closely.

Training and Awareness: Employees should be educated on access control policies and best practices to ensure they understand their roles in maintaining security.

Physical Access Controls: Physical access to facilities housing critical IT infrastructure should also be controlled, with measures such as badge access, biometric scanners, and surveillance systems.

Cloud Access Control: In cloud environments, organizations should implement access controls specific to the cloud provider's services and resources.

Implementing strong access controls is an ongoing process that requires collaboration between IT, security teams, and other stakeholders. It involves defining and documenting policies, configuring access control mechanisms, and regularly reviewing and updating them. Additionally, organizations should conduct periodic access control assessments and security audits to identify and address vulnerabilities and compliance gaps.

It's important to strike a balance between security and usability when implementing access controls. Overly restrictive controls can hinder productivity, while insufficient controls can expose the organization to security risks. Therefore, access control strategies should be tailored to the organization's unique needs and risks.

In summary, access controls are a cornerstone of modern cybersecurity. They protect sensitive data, mitigate risks, and ensure compliance with regulations. By implementing strong access controls, organizations can fortify their defenses and maintain the confidentiality, integrity, and availability of their digital assets.

BOOK 4
WEB APP SCANNING MASTERY
EXPERT TECHNIQUES FOR RED TEAM SPECIALISTS

ROB BOTWRIGHT

Chapter 1: Fundamentals of Web Application Security

The Open Web Application Security Project (OWASP) is a trusted source of information and guidance when it comes to web application security. Their "Top Ten" project highlights the most critical web application security risks facing organizations today. Understanding these vulnerabilities is crucial for anyone involved in developing or maintaining web applications, as well as for those responsible for their security.

The OWASP Top Ten list is a valuable resource because it is updated periodically to reflect the evolving threat landscape. This ensures that it remains relevant and addresses emerging security challenges. Now, let's delve into the OWASP Top Ten vulnerabilities, starting with the first one on the list.

Injection: Injection attacks, such as SQL injection, occur when an attacker inserts malicious code into input fields, which can then manipulate or compromise the application's database. These attacks can lead to data breaches, unauthorized access, or even complete system compromise.

Broken Authentication: Weaknesses in authentication and session management can allow attackers to gain unauthorized access to user accounts. This includes issues like weak passwords, insecure session management, and the lack of multi-factor authentication.

Sensitive Data Exposure: Failure to properly protect sensitive data, like credit card numbers or personal information, can result in data breaches. Encryption, access controls, and secure storage practices are crucial in preventing this vulnerability.

XML External Entities (XXE): XXE attacks occur when an application processes XML input from untrusted sources without proper validation. Attackers can exploit this vulnerability to read files on the server or launch denial-of-service attacks.

Broken Access Control: This vulnerability allows attackers to bypass authorization and access resources or perform actions they shouldn't be able to. Properly defining and enforcing access controls is essential to mitigate this risk.

Security Misconfigurations: Misconfigured settings, such as default credentials, unnecessary features, or overly permissive permissions, can open the door to attacks. Regular security reviews and automated scanning tools can help identify and fix misconfigurations.

Cross-Site Scripting (XSS): XSS attacks occur when an attacker injects malicious scripts into web pages viewed by other users. This can lead to theft of session cookies, redirecting users to malicious sites, or defacement of web pages.

Insecure Deserialization: This vulnerability involves attackers manipulating the deserialization process to execute arbitrary code or launch attacks. Properly validating and sanitizing serialized data is essential to prevent this risk.

Using Components with Known Vulnerabilities: Many applications rely on third-party components, and if those components have known vulnerabilities, attackers can exploit them. Regularly updating and patching libraries and dependencies is critical.

Insufficient Logging and Monitoring: Failing to log and monitor security events makes it difficult to detect and respond to attacks. Proper logging, real-time monitoring, and incident response plans are vital components of a robust security strategy.

Understanding and addressing these vulnerabilities is not only a matter of compliance but also a critical step in safeguarding applications and sensitive data. By staying informed about the OWASP Top Ten and following best practices for secure development and deployment, organizations can reduce their risk of falling victim to common web application attacks. Security is an ongoing process, and it requires a proactive and collaborative effort from development, operations, and security teams to mitigate these risks effectively.

Web application architecture is the foundation upon which modern web applications are built, and understanding its basics is crucial for developers, architects, and anyone involved in web development. At its core, web application architecture defines the structure, components, and interactions of a web application, providing a blueprint for building scalable, reliable, and secure applications. Let's explore the fundamental concepts of web application architecture to gain a deeper understanding of how web applications work.

At the heart of any web application is the client-server model. This model involves two main components: the client, which is typically a web browser, and the server, which stores and processes data and serves web pages. The client and server communicate over the internet using standardized protocols, primarily HTTP (Hypertext Transfer Protocol).

Web applications follow a request-response model, where the client sends requests to the server, and the server responds with the requested data. These requests can be for various resources, such as web pages, images, videos, or data from a database. When you enter a URL in your web browser and press Enter, your browser sends an HTTP request to the server hosting the web application.

Web applications often consist of multiple layers or components that work together to deliver the desired functionality. The most common layers in a web application architecture are the presentation layer, application layer, and data layer. The presentation layer is responsible for the user interface and rendering web pages for the client. It includes HTML, CSS, and JavaScript code that runs in the user's browser.

The application layer contains the business logic of the web application. This is where data processing, user authentication, and other core functionalities are implemented. Developers write server-side code using programming languages like Python, Ruby, Java, or JavaScript (Node.js) to build the application logic. The application layer often interfaces with the data layer to retrieve and store data.

The data layer is where data is stored, retrieved, and managed. It typically involves databases, which can be relational (e.g., MySQL, PostgreSQL) or NoSQL (e.g., MongoDB, Redis), depending on the application's requirements. Data is stored in a structured manner, and the application layer interacts with the database to perform operations like reading, writing, updating, and deleting data.

Web applications often incorporate additional components for scalability, performance, and security. One common addition is a web server, responsible for handling incoming HTTP requests and routing them to the appropriate components within the application. Popular web servers include Apache, Nginx, and Microsoft Internet Information Services (IIS).

Caching mechanisms can also be employed to improve performance. Caching involves storing frequently accessed data or web pages in a temporary storage location, such as memory, to reduce the need to retrieve them from the database or generate them dynamically.

Load balancers distribute incoming traffic across multiple servers to ensure high availability and even distribution of the workload. This is especially important for web applications with heavy traffic, as it prevents a single server from becoming a bottleneck.

In a distributed web application architecture, microservices have gained popularity. Microservices involve breaking down the application into small, independent services that can be developed, deployed, and scaled separately. Each microservice is responsible for a specific function or feature, allowing for greater flexibility and scalability.

Web application security is a critical consideration. Security measures should be implemented at every layer of the architecture to protect against common threats such as SQL injection, cross-site scripting (XSS), and cross-site request forgery (CSRF). Authentication and authorization mechanisms should be in place to ensure that only authorized users can access certain resources or perform specific actions.

Scalability is another key aspect of web application architecture. As web traffic grows, the application must be able to handle increased load without sacrificing performance. Horizontal scaling involves adding more servers to distribute the load, while vertical scaling involves upgrading individual servers with more resources. Web application architecture can vary greatly depending on the specific requirements of the application. Some applications are designed for simplicity and ease of development, while others prioritize performance, scalability, and security. The choice of architecture depends on factors like the expected user traffic, the complexity of the application, and the available resources.

In summary, web application architecture is a fundamental concept in web development. Understanding its basics, including the client-server model, layers, components, and additional considerations such as security and scalability, is essential for building robust and effective web applications. As technology continues to evolve, web application architecture will continue to adapt and incorporate new techniques and tools to meet the ever-changing demands of the digital world.

Chapter 2: Advanced Web App Reconnaissance

Information gathering and footprinting are critical initial steps in the process of ethical hacking and penetration testing.

Before attempting any attack or exploitation, it's essential to gather as much information as possible about the target system or organization. This process allows security professionals to understand the potential vulnerabilities and weaknesses that may exist, helping them make informed decisions and prioritize their efforts.

Footprinting involves the systematic collection of information about an organization, its infrastructure, and its digital presence. This can include details about the organization's domain names, IP addresses, network architecture, and more.

The primary goal of footprinting is to build a comprehensive profile of the target, giving the ethical hacker or penetration tester a clear understanding of the organization's digital landscape.

One common technique used in information gathering is passive reconnaissance. This approach involves collecting data without directly interacting with the target.

Passive reconnaissance methods include searching for publicly available information using search engines like Google or Bing. Ethical hackers can use advanced search operators and specific queries to find hidden information, such as sensitive documents or exposed directories.

Another passive reconnaissance method involves examining the target's social media profiles and online presence. Employees of an organization may inadvertently leak information about their workplace or reveal details about the organization's internal operations.

Additionally, passive reconnaissance can include searching for information on public forums, job postings, or news articles related to the organization. Ethical hackers often look for any breadcrumbs of information that can help them piece together a more comprehensive picture of the target.

While passive reconnaissance is valuable, it may not provide all the necessary information needed for a successful attack. In such cases, active reconnaissance techniques can be employed.

Active reconnaissance involves directly interacting with the target to gather information. This approach is riskier because it can trigger security alerts or leave traces of the probing activity.

One common active reconnaissance technique is DNS (Domain Name System) enumeration. By querying DNS servers, ethical hackers can discover additional domain names associated with the target organization, potentially revealing new targets or attack vectors.

Another active reconnaissance method is port scanning. Ethical hackers use specialized tools to scan the target's IP addresses and check which ports are open and accessible.

Knowing which ports are open is crucial because it helps determine which services are running on the target systems. These services can be potential points of entry for attackers.

Banner grabbing is often used in conjunction with port scanning. It involves connecting to open ports and retrieving information from the service banners or banners.

Service banners can reveal valuable details about the software and versions running on the target system, which is crucial for identifying potential vulnerabilities or weaknesses.

Reverse IP lookup is another active reconnaissance technique. This involves discovering other websites hosted on the same web server as the target site.

Finding other websites on the same server can provide insights into shared hosting environments, potential vulnerabilities, or dependencies that may exist.

During the reconnaissance phase, ethical hackers also focus on social engineering.

Social engineering is the practice of manipulating individuals into divulging confidential information or performing actions that compromise security.

Attackers may impersonate employees, contractors, or trusted individuals to gather sensitive information. It's crucial for ethical hackers to understand the social engineering techniques attackers might use and help organizations protect against them.

Footprinting also extends to email systems. Ethical hackers may investigate email servers and domains associated with the target organization.

Email footprinting can uncover email addresses, mail exchange (MX) records, and other critical information that attackers could use to launch email-based attacks such as phishing or spear-phishing.

When conducting information gathering and footprinting, ethical hackers should consider the legal and ethical aspects of their activities.

Obtaining information without proper authorization or engaging in intrusive reconnaissance can have legal consequences.

Additionally, ethical hackers should follow a structured and documented approach, recording all the information they gather and the methods they use.

This documentation is essential for later stages of penetration testing, as it helps ethical hackers identify potential vulnerabilities and plan their testing strategy.

In summary, information gathering and footprinting are essential initial steps in ethical hacking and penetration testing.

These activities provide ethical hackers with a comprehensive understanding of the target organization's digital landscape, helping them identify potential vulnerabilities and weaknesses.

Whether using passive or active reconnaissance techniques, ethical hackers must approach these activities with a strong ethical and legal framework.

By following a structured and documented approach, ethical hackers can contribute to improving an organization's security posture while ensuring they adhere to ethical and legal standards.

Mapping the structure and assets of an application is a crucial step in the process of understanding its architecture and potential vulnerabilities.

This mapping process involves creating a detailed inventory of the various components and resources that make up the application.

One of the first steps in mapping an application's structure is to identify its different layers.

Applications often consist of multiple layers, including the presentation layer, the application logic layer, and the data storage layer.

By understanding these layers, ethical hackers gain insights into the flow of data and interactions within the application.

In addition to identifying layers, ethical hackers need to identify the technologies and frameworks used in the application.

This information can help them better understand the potential attack vectors and vulnerabilities associated with specific technologies.

Next, ethical hackers should map out the application's user interface (UI) and its functionality.

This involves identifying the various web pages or screens that users interact with and the actions they can perform.

Mapping the UI and functionality helps ethical hackers identify potential security flaws, such as input validation issues or insecure data transmission.

In addition to the UI, ethical hackers should also map out the application's APIs (Application Programming Interfaces).

APIs are essential for communication between different parts of the application and with external services.

Understanding the APIs used by the application can help ethical hackers identify potential vulnerabilities related to authentication, authorization, and data exposure.

Another critical aspect of mapping an application is identifying the data flows and data storage mechanisms.

Ethical hackers need to trace how data moves through the application, where it's stored, and how it's accessed.

This information can reveal potential data leakage points and areas where sensitive information might be at risk.

While mapping the application's structure, ethical hackers should also consider the potential threat modeling.

This involves thinking like an attacker and identifying possible attack scenarios and vectors based on the application's architecture and functionality.

By conducting threat modeling during the mapping phase, ethical hackers can proactively identify and address security risks.

Once the application's structure and assets are mapped out, ethical hackers can move on to the next step: identifying potential vulnerabilities.

This involves looking for weaknesses in the application's design, code, and configurations that could be exploited by attackers.

Common vulnerabilities to look for during this phase include input validation issues, authentication and authorization flaws, and insecure data storage practices. Ethical hackers should also pay attention to any third-party components or libraries used by the application, as vulnerabilities in these components can pose significant risks.

In addition to identifying vulnerabilities, ethical hackers should assess the application's security controls and defenses.

This includes evaluating the effectiveness of measures such as access controls, encryption, and logging.

Ethical hackers may also perform security assessments, such as penetration testing or code reviews, to uncover specific vulnerabilities.

Throughout the mapping and assessment process, ethical hackers should maintain detailed documentation of their findings.

This documentation is essential for reporting vulnerabilities to the organization and for helping developers and security teams address and remediate the issues.

Effective communication with the organization's stakeholders is a critical aspect of ethical hacking.

Ethical hackers should provide clear and actionable recommendations for mitigating the identified vulnerabilities.

They should also prioritize vulnerabilities based on their potential impact and likelihood of exploitation.

In some cases, ethical hackers may need to collaborate with the organization's development and IT teams to address and remediate vulnerabilities.

Mapping the application's structure and assets is an ongoing process, as applications evolve over time.

Ethical hackers should periodically revisit their mapping efforts to ensure that they stay up to date with any changes or additions to the application.

In summary, mapping the structure and assets of an application is a fundamental step in the ethical hacking process.

It involves identifying the layers, technologies, UI, APIs, data flows, and potential vulnerabilities within the application.

By conducting a thorough mapping, ethical hackers can better understand the application's architecture and help organizations improve their security posture.

Effective communication and documentation are essential throughout this process, ensuring that vulnerabilities are addressed and mitigated promptly.

Chapter 3: In-Depth Web App Scanning Tools

Web vulnerability scanners are essential tools for identifying security weaknesses in web applications and websites.

These scanners automate the process of identifying vulnerabilities, making it easier for security professionals to detect and remediate issues.

There are various web vulnerability scanners available in the market, each with its own set of features and capabilities.

In this section, we will compare and contrast some of the most popular web vulnerability scanners to help you choose the right one for your needs.

One of the widely used web vulnerability scanners is Burp Suite by PortSwigger.

Burp Suite offers a comprehensive set of features, including both manual and automated scanning capabilities.

It provides a user-friendly interface, making it suitable for both beginners and experienced security testers.

Burp Suite can identify various vulnerabilities, such as SQL injection, cross-site scripting (XSS), and more.

Another popular web vulnerability scanner is OWASP ZAP (Zed Attack Proxy).

ZAP is an open-source tool developed by the OWASP community.

It offers automated scanning and advanced features for experienced testers.

ZAP is known for its active community and frequent updates, which ensure it stays up to date with the latest threats and vulnerabilities.

Acunetix is another notable web vulnerability scanner known for its accuracy and speed.

It provides a robust set of features for scanning web applications and APIs.

Acunetix can detect a wide range of vulnerabilities, including those related to authentication, authorization, and input validation.

Nessus, developed by Tenable, is a versatile vulnerability scanner that can be used for network and web application scanning.

It offers a large database of plugins and a comprehensive reporting system.

Nessus can identify vulnerabilities in web applications, web servers, and underlying infrastructure.

Nexpose, by Rapid7, is a vulnerability management solution that includes web application scanning capabilities.

It provides asset discovery, vulnerability assessment, and remediation workflows.

Nexpose is suitable for organizations looking for an integrated solution to manage their security vulnerabilities.

Qualys Web Application Scanning (WAS) is part of the Qualys Cloud Platform and focuses on web application security.

It offers automated scanning, detailed reports, and integration with other Qualys security solutions.

Qualys WAS is a scalable option for organizations of all sizes.

Now that we have introduced some of the popular web vulnerability scanners, let's compare them based on several key factors.

First, let's consider the ease of use.

Burp Suite and OWASP ZAP are known for their user-friendly interfaces and are suitable for security professionals of all levels.

Acunetix and Nessus also provide user-friendly interfaces, but they may require more experience to fully utilize their advanced features.

Nexpose and Qualys WAS are designed with scalability in mind, making them suitable for larger organizations with complex environments.

Next, let's look at the types of vulnerabilities these scanners can detect.

Burp Suite, Acunetix, and Nessus are known for their comprehensive vulnerability detection capabilities.

They can identify a wide range of vulnerabilities, from common to advanced ones.

OWASP ZAP, being open source, benefits from a strong community and frequent updates, ensuring it can detect the latest vulnerabilities.

Nexpose and Qualys WAS focus not only on web application vulnerabilities but also on overall vulnerability management, making them suitable for organizations with diverse security needs.

Scanning speed is another important consideration.

Burp Suite, Acunetix, and Nessus are known for their fast scanning speeds, allowing security professionals to assess web applications quickly.

OWASP ZAP's scanning speed depends on the complexity of the application and the depth of the scan.

Nexpose and Qualys WAS are designed for larger-scale scanning, so their speed may vary depending on the organization's infrastructure.

Integration capabilities are crucial for organizations that want to streamline their security processes.

Burp Suite, Acunetix, and Nessus offer integration options with various security tools and platforms.

OWASP ZAP's open-source nature allows for customization and integration with other tools.

Nexpose and Qualys WAS provide integration with other Qualys solutions, creating a comprehensive security ecosystem.

Finally, let's consider the cost and licensing models.

Burp Suite, Acunetix, and Nessus offer different pricing tiers, including free versions with limited features and paid versions with more capabilities.

OWASP ZAP is open source and free to use, making it a cost-effective choice for organizations with budget constraints.

Nexpose and Qualys WAS follow a subscription-based pricing model, which may be more suitable for larger organizations with specific security requirements.

In summary, choosing the right web vulnerability scanner depends on various factors, including your organization's size, budget, and specific security needs.

Burp Suite, Acunetix, Nessus, OWASP ZAP, Nexpose, and Qualys WAS are all reputable options with their own strengths and weaknesses.

Evaluate each scanner based on your unique requirements to ensure you select the one that best aligns with your security goals.

Remember that an effective web vulnerability scanner is an essential tool in maintaining the security and integrity of your web applications and websites.

Configuring and using Burp Suite is a fundamental skill for web application security professionals.

Burp Suite is a powerful web vulnerability scanner and penetration testing tool that helps identify and mitigate security issues in web applications.

In this section, we will explore how to configure and effectively use Burp Suite to enhance the security of web applications.

First, let's start with the initial setup of Burp Suite.

After downloading and installing Burp Suite, you'll want to configure your proxy settings.

Burp Suite operates as a proxy between your browser and the web application you are testing, so it's essential to configure your browser to use Burp Suite as a proxy.

Typically, you set up your browser to use the Burp Suite proxy by specifying the proxy address and port.

Once your browser is configured to use Burp Suite as a proxy, you can start intercepting and inspecting HTTP requests and responses.

This interception capability is at the core of Burp Suite's functionality, allowing you to analyze and manipulate web traffic.

Next, you'll need to configure Burp Suite's proxy listener settings.

You can access this by navigating to the "Proxy" tab and clicking on the "Options" sub-tab.

Here, you can specify the listening host and port for Burp Suite.

By default, Burp Suite listens on localhost (127.0.0.1) and port 8080, but you can change these settings based on your preferences and requirements.

Now, let's discuss some common use cases for Burp Suite.

One of the primary uses of Burp Suite is to intercept and inspect HTTP requests and responses.

When you visit a web application in your browser, Burp Suite intercepts the traffic, allowing you to view and modify the data being sent between your browser and the web server.

This interception feature is invaluable for identifying vulnerabilities such as Cross-Site Scripting (XSS) or SQL Injection.

Burp Suite also offers an intruder tool, which allows you to automate various types of attacks against a web application.

You can define attack payloads and customize attack parameters, making it a versatile tool for testing different attack vectors.

Intruder can help identify vulnerabilities like Brute Force, Directory Traversal, and more.

Another essential tool within Burp Suite is the scanner.

The scanner automates the process of identifying security vulnerabilities by sending specially crafted requests to the target application and analyzing the responses for signs of vulnerabilities.

This feature can detect a wide range of vulnerabilities, including SQL Injection, Cross-Site Scripting, and more.

Burp Suite also provides a repeater tool that allows you to send individual HTTP requests and observe the responses.

This is useful for manually testing and modifying requests to see how the application responds.

The repeater tool is handy for fine-tuning payloads and verifying vulnerabilities discovered during scanning.

Furthermore, Burp Suite includes a spider tool that can crawl a web application, following links and mapping out the application's structure.

This helps in identifying hidden pages and potential vulnerabilities.

Another noteworthy feature is the Burp Collaborator, which assists in detecting blind vulnerabilities such as Blind SQL Injection or Blind SSRF.

Burp Collaborator creates unique payloads and tracks interactions with external services, providing evidence of potential vulnerabilities.

As you work with Burp Suite, it's important to customize your configuration to suit your specific testing needs.

You can configure your target scope, which defines the scope of your testing, ensuring that you only test the intended application and not external sites.

Additionally, you can configure various options for handling cookies, authentication, and session management.

In the "Target" tab, you can define your target scope, and in the "Session" tab, you can manage your sessions and configure authentication settings.

Burp Suite also supports extensions, which allow you to extend its functionality.

There is a vibrant community of security professionals who develop and share Burp Suite extensions, providing additional features and capabilities.

Extensions can be used to automate tasks, enhance scanning, and integrate Burp Suite with other tools and platforms.

Lastly, it's crucial to stay up-to-date with the latest version of Burp Suite.

The developers regularly release updates that include bug fixes, new features, and improved security checks.

By keeping your Burp Suite installation current, you ensure that you have access to the latest tools and capabilities for securing web applications.

In summary, Burp Suite is a versatile and powerful tool for web application security testing.

Configuring and using Burp Suite effectively is essential for identifying and mitigating security vulnerabilities in web applications.

By understanding its features and capabilities, you can enhance the security posture of your web applications and protect against a wide range of threats.

Chapter 4: Automated Vulnerability Assessment

Automated scanning techniques are a crucial component of modern cybersecurity efforts.

These techniques leverage automated tools and software to identify vulnerabilities and weaknesses in computer systems, networks, and applications.

The primary goal of automated scanning is to detect security issues efficiently and accurately, reducing the manual effort required to assess an organization's security posture.

Automated scanning tools, often referred to as vulnerability scanners, are designed to simulate the actions of a malicious attacker.

They scan target systems, networks, or applications, looking for known vulnerabilities and misconfigurations that could be exploited by cybercriminals.

One of the significant advantages of automated scanning is its speed and scalability.

These tools can assess a large number of systems or applications in a relatively short amount of time, making them invaluable for organizations with extensive IT infrastructure.

Additionally, automated scanning helps organizations maintain continuous monitoring of their security posture, as scans can be scheduled to run regularly.

One of the fundamental principles of automated scanning is that it relies on a database of known vulnerabilities.

This database, often referred to as a vulnerability signature database, contains information about specific vulnerabilities, including their characteristics, severity levels, and potential impact.

When a vulnerability scanner conducts a scan, it compares the characteristics of the target system or application with the information in the database to identify potential vulnerabilities.

Automated scanning tools are categorized into two main types: network vulnerability scanners and web application scanners.

Network vulnerability scanners focus on assessing the security of an organization's network infrastructure.

They scan devices such as servers, routers, firewalls, and switches for vulnerabilities that could be exploited by an attacker to gain unauthorized access or disrupt network services.

Web application scanners, on the other hand, are designed specifically to assess the security of web applications and websites.

They analyze web application code, inputs, and configurations to identify common web-related vulnerabilities like Cross-Site Scripting (XSS), SQL Injection, and Cross-Site Request Forgery (CSRF).

Some advanced scanning tools can perform both network and web application scans, providing comprehensive security assessments.

One of the key challenges in automated scanning is managing false positives and false negatives.

False positives occur when a scanner incorrectly identifies a non-existent vulnerability, potentially leading to wasted time and resources.

False negatives, on the other hand, are instances where a scanner fails to detect a genuine vulnerability, leaving the organization exposed to potential security risks.

To mitigate false positives and false negatives, organizations need to fine-tune their scanning tools and configure them to match their specific environment and requirements.

This involves adjusting scan settings, excluding known false positives, and ensuring that the scanner is up-to-date with the latest vulnerability signatures.

Another important consideration in automated scanning is compliance requirements.

Many regulatory frameworks and industry standards, such as the Payment Card Industry Data Security Standard (PCI DSS) and the Health Insurance Portability and Accountability Act (HIPAA), mandate regular security scans and vulnerability assessments.

Automated scanning tools can help organizations meet these compliance requirements by providing evidence of their security efforts.

Moreover, automated scanning can be integrated into a broader security management program that includes incident response, patch management, and risk assessment.

Automated scanning tools are often used in combination with other security technologies and practices to create a robust defense against cyber threats.

For example, organizations can use intrusion detection systems (IDS) and intrusion prevention systems (IPS) to detect and block potential attacks in real-time based on the vulnerabilities identified by scanning tools.

Additionally, automated scanning can inform patch management processes, helping organizations prioritize and deploy critical security patches to mitigate identified vulnerabilities.

In some cases, automated scanning can be integrated with security information and event management (SIEM) systems to provide a comprehensive view of an organization's security posture and to enable faster incident response.

It's important to note that automated scanning is just one part of an effective cybersecurity strategy.

While these tools can identify known vulnerabilities, they cannot detect novel or zero-day vulnerabilities for which no known signature exists.

Therefore, organizations must complement automated scanning with other security measures, such as network segmentation, access controls, and user education, to reduce their overall risk exposure.

Furthermore, scanning should be conducted in a controlled and authorized manner to avoid unintentional disruption of services or systems.

Unauthorized or uncontrolled scanning can lead to network congestion, service outages, or even legal repercussions.

In summary, automated scanning techniques are essential tools in the cybersecurity arsenal, enabling organizations to efficiently and systematically assess their security posture.

These tools play a vital role in identifying known vulnerabilities and misconfigurations that could be exploited by cybercriminals.

However, organizations must use automated scanning in conjunction with other security practices to create a comprehensive defense against a wide range of cyber threats.

Interpretation of scan results is a critical phase in the vulnerability assessment and risk management process.

Once an automated scanning tool has conducted a security scan, the next step is to analyze and interpret the results to understand the implications for an organization's security posture.

The interpretation of scan results involves identifying vulnerabilities, assessing their severity, and determining the appropriate remediation actions.

Vulnerabilities are weaknesses or flaws in a system, network, or application that could be exploited by malicious actors to compromise security.

These vulnerabilities may range from minor misconfigurations to critical flaws that pose significant risks to an organization's assets and data.

Upon completion of a scan, a list of vulnerabilities is typically generated by the scanning tool, along with detailed information about each one.

This information includes the name of the vulnerability, a description of the issue, its severity level, and any potential impact it may have on the target system or application.

Severity levels are often categorized as critical, high, medium, and low, providing a way to prioritize remediation efforts based on the perceived risk.

Critical vulnerabilities are those that pose an immediate and severe threat to the security of the target, while low-severity vulnerabilities represent a lower risk.

To effectively interpret scan results, organizations should establish a consistent process for vulnerability management.

This process includes assigning responsibility for reviewing and prioritizing vulnerabilities, as well as defining the criteria for classifying and addressing them.

A common approach to prioritizing vulnerabilities is to use the Common Vulnerability Scoring System (CVSS), which assigns a numerical score to each vulnerability based on its characteristics.

The CVSS score takes into account factors such as the ease of exploitation, the potential impact, and whether there are known exploits available in the wild.

By using CVSS scores, organizations can objectively assess the severity of vulnerabilities and make informed decisions about which ones to address first.

During the interpretation phase, it's essential to distinguish between confirmed vulnerabilities and potential false positives.

False positives occur when a scanning tool incorrectly identifies a non-existent vulnerability, leading to unnecessary concern and resource allocation.

To minimize false positives, organizations should validate the findings by conducting manual assessments or additional testing.

Once vulnerabilities are confirmed, the next step is to prioritize remediation efforts.

This involves assessing the potential impact of each vulnerability on the organization's assets and operations.

For example, a critical vulnerability that could result in data breaches or system compromise should take precedence over lower-severity issues.

Organizations must also consider the availability of patches or fixes for the vulnerabilities.

In many cases, software vendors release security updates or patches to address known vulnerabilities.

If patches are available, organizations should prioritize their deployment to mitigate the risk quickly.

However, not all vulnerabilities have patches readily available, especially zero-day vulnerabilities for which no official fixes exist.

In such cases, organizations may need to implement compensating controls, temporary workarounds, or other mitigation strategies to reduce the risk until a patch is available.

Furthermore, interpreting scan results should take into account the organization's specific risk tolerance and business priorities.

Some vulnerabilities may be acceptable if they are deemed low-risk and have a minimal impact on critical systems.

In contrast, vulnerabilities affecting mission-critical systems or those with sensitive data may require immediate attention, regardless of their severity.

The interpretation of scan results should also consider the organization's compliance requirements and industry standards.

Regulatory bodies and industry-specific regulations often mandate the timely remediation of certain vulnerabilities to maintain compliance.

For instance, the Payment Card Industry Data Security Standard (PCI DSS) requires organizations handling credit card data to address vulnerabilities promptly to protect cardholder information.

Additionally, interpreting scan results should involve communication with relevant stakeholders, including IT teams, system administrators, and management.

Clear and transparent communication is essential to ensure that all parties understand the significance of the vulnerabilities and the proposed remediation actions.

Stakeholders should collaborate to develop a remediation plan that aligns with the organization's priorities and resources.

Furthermore, organizations should establish a mechanism for tracking and monitoring the progress of vulnerability remediation efforts.

This may involve the use of a centralized vulnerability management system or a tracking tool that allows the organization to monitor the status of each vulnerability, from identification to resolution.

Finally, the interpretation of scan results should be an ongoing process, rather than a one-time activity.

Security threats and vulnerabilities evolve continuously, so organizations must regularly conduct scans, assess results, and adjust their remediation strategies accordingly.

Continuous monitoring and proactive vulnerability management are key to maintaining a robust security posture in the face of evolving threats.

In summary, the interpretation of scan results is a critical aspect of effective vulnerability management and risk mitigation.

It involves identifying vulnerabilities, assessing their severity, and prioritizing remediation efforts based on the organization's risk tolerance and business priorities.

Clear communication with stakeholders, compliance considerations, and ongoing monitoring are essential components of the interpretation process, ensuring that organizations can effectively address security vulnerabilities and protect their assets and data.

Chapter 5: Manual Testing and Exploitation

Manual SQL injection testing is a crucial aspect of web application security assessment.

Unlike automated tools that can identify common vulnerabilities, manual testing allows security professionals to explore and exploit SQL injection vulnerabilities in a more controlled and comprehensive manner.

SQL injection is a type of security vulnerability that occurs when an attacker can manipulate the SQL queries sent to a database through a web application.

This manipulation can result in unauthorized access to the database, data leakage, data manipulation, and even full control over the application and the underlying database.

Manual SQL injection testing typically begins with reconnaissance and information gathering.

Security professionals need to understand the target web application, its structure, and the parameters that may be susceptible to SQL injection.

They also need to identify the database management system (DBMS) being used, as different DBMSs may require different SQL injection techniques.

Once the initial reconnaissance is complete, testers proceed to analyze the application's input points, such as form fields, URL parameters, and cookies, to identify potential injection points.

For example, a login form that accepts a username and password might be a likely candidate for SQL injection.

Once potential injection points are identified, testers aim to inject SQL code into these input fields.

The goal is to manipulate the SQL query in a way that it returns unintended data or performs unauthorized actions.

A simple example of SQL injection is appending a single-quote character (') to a username input field, which may lead to an error message or unexpected behavior if the application is vulnerable.

Testers then progress to more complex attacks, such as UNION-based and blind SQL injection, where they attempt to extract sensitive data from the database.

In a UNION-based attack, testers inject a SQL statement that combines the results of the original query with their own query, allowing them to retrieve data from other database tables.

Blind SQL injection, on the other hand, relies on the application's response to infer whether the injected query is true or false.

Testers use techniques like Boolean-based and time-based blind SQL injection to extract data character by character.

To mitigate the risk of causing damage to the target application or database during testing, testers often employ sandboxed or controlled environments.

These environments replicate the target system, allowing testers to safely conduct SQL injection testing without impacting production systems.

While performing manual SQL injection testing, testers should document their findings meticulously.

This documentation includes details of the injection points, the SQL injection payloads used, the responses received, and any potential vulnerabilities discovered.

This information is essential for later analysis, reporting, and remediation.

Testers should also be aware of ethical considerations during manual SQL injection testing.

Unauthorized access or data manipulation can have legal and ethical implications, so it's crucial to obtain proper authorization and conduct testing within the boundaries defined by the organization.

Furthermore, testers must exercise caution to avoid causing harm to the target system or exposing sensitive information.

Once manual SQL injection testing is complete, testers should report their findings to the organization's security and development teams.

This report typically includes a detailed description of the vulnerabilities, proof-of-concept examples, and recommendations for remediation.

The development team can then use this information to fix the vulnerabilities and enhance the application's security.

It's essential for organizations to address SQL injection vulnerabilities promptly, as they pose a significant risk to data confidentiality and application integrity.

Regular security testing, including manual SQL injection testing, should be integrated into the software development lifecycle to proactively identify and remediate vulnerabilities.

In addition to identifying vulnerabilities, manual SQL injection testing helps organizations understand the impact of potential attacks.

By simulating real-world attack scenarios, testers can demonstrate the risks associated with SQL injection and the potential consequences of a successful exploitation.

This information can be used to educate development teams, management, and stakeholders about the importance of secure coding practices and the need for ongoing security testing.

Manual SQL injection testing also plays a crucial role in compliance with industry standards and regulations.

Many regulatory frameworks, such as the Payment Card Industry Data Security Standard (PCI DSS) and the General Data Protection Regulation (GDPR), require organizations to protect sensitive data and regularly test for vulnerabilities.

Failure to address SQL injection vulnerabilities can lead to data breaches, financial losses, and reputational damage.

In summary, manual SQL injection testing is a vital component of web application security assessment.

It allows security professionals to identify, exploit, and report SQL injection vulnerabilities in a controlled and comprehensive manner.

This testing helps organizations understand the risks associated with SQL injection, educate their teams, and comply with regulatory requirements.

By integrating manual SQL injection testing into their security practices, organizations can enhance the security of their web applications and protect sensitive data from unauthorized access and manipulation.

Exploiting Cross-Site Scripting (XSS) vulnerabilities is a critical topic in the realm of web application security.

XSS is a type of security vulnerability that allows attackers to inject malicious scripts into web pages viewed by other users.

These scripts can execute in the context of the victim's browser, potentially stealing sensitive data, hijacking user sessions, defacing websites, and spreading malware.

Understanding how XSS works and how to exploit it is essential for both security professionals and developers to protect web applications effectively.

XSS vulnerabilities typically occur when web applications include untrusted data in web pages sent to users.

This untrusted data can come from various sources, such as user input, data retrieved from databases, or external APIs.

If the application fails to properly validate and sanitize this data before rendering it in web pages, it becomes susceptible to XSS attacks.

There are several types of XSS vulnerabilities, with the most common being Stored, Reflected, and DOM-based XSS.

Stored XSS occurs when an attacker injects malicious scripts into a web application's database.

These scripts are then retrieved and executed when other users view the affected page, making it a potent vector for stealing sensitive data or performing attacks on behalf of the victim.

Reflected XSS, on the other hand, involves injecting malicious scripts into a URL or a web form.

When a user clicks on a malicious link or submits a form with the injected data, the script executes in their browser, allowing the attacker to steal cookies, impersonate users, or perform other malicious actions.

DOM-based XSS relies on the Document Object Model (DOM) of a web page.

In this case, the attacker manipulates the DOM directly by injecting scripts that are processed by the victim's browser, leading to unintended behaviors and potential security breaches.

To exploit XSS vulnerabilities, attackers craft malicious payloads that can execute arbitrary code in the context of a user's session.

These payloads often include JavaScript code that can perform actions such as stealing cookies, sending user data to a remote server, or redirecting users to malicious websites.

One common technique is to steal a user's session cookie, which can grant the attacker access to the victim's account.

Once an attacker has identified a vulnerable input field or URL parameter, they inject their malicious payload.

For instance, if a website allows users to submit comments and doesn't properly sanitize the input, an attacker can inject a comment containing a malicious script.

When other users view the comments section, the script executes in their browsers, potentially compromising their sessions.

Exploiting XSS vulnerabilities also requires an understanding of how to obfuscate payloads to evade detection by security mechanisms, such as web application firewalls (WAFs) or browser security features.

Attackers may use techniques like encoding, concatenation, or using character substitutions to hide their malicious code from automated scanners.

Additionally, attackers may employ JavaScript tricks and evasion techniques to execute their payloads without raising suspicion.

These tricks can include bypassing filters, escaping special characters, or evading content security policies (CSPs).

XSS attacks can have severe consequences for both web applications and their users.

They can lead to data breaches, identity theft, financial losses, and damage to an organization's reputation.

To mitigate the risk of XSS vulnerabilities, developers must follow secure coding practices.

This includes validating and sanitizing user input, implementing proper output encoding, and using security mechanisms like CSPs to restrict the execution of scripts.

Web application security scanners and penetration testers also play a crucial role in identifying and remediating XSS vulnerabilities.

When exploiting XSS vulnerabilities, ethical hackers aim to demonstrate the impact of a successful attack to organizations.

They can use payloads to steal session cookies, redirect users to malicious websites, or simulate defacement to emphasize the importance of security measures.

However, it's essential to obtain proper authorization before conducting any security testing on web applications.

Exploiting XSS vulnerabilities without permission can lead to legal consequences.

After successfully exploiting XSS vulnerabilities, security professionals document their findings and provide recommendations for remediation to the organization's development and security teams.

This documentation helps developers understand the nature of the vulnerability and how to fix it properly.

Developers can implement patches or code fixes to prevent similar vulnerabilities from occurring in the future.

Regular security testing, including automated scanning and manual testing for XSS vulnerabilities, should be part of an organization's security strategy to proactively identify and address such risks.

Furthermore, organizations should educate their development teams about secure coding practices and the importance of validating and sanitizing user input.

In summary, exploiting Cross-Site Scripting (XSS) vulnerabilities is a critical aspect of web application security.

Understanding how these vulnerabilities work and how attackers can exploit them is essential for both security professionals and developers.

By following secure coding practices, conducting regular security testing, and educating teams, organizations can effectively mitigate the risk of XSS vulnerabilities and protect their web applications and users from potential harm.

Chapter 6: API Security Testing

Understanding API authentication is fundamental in the world of modern software development and web services.

APIs, or Application Programming Interfaces, enable different software systems to communicate and interact with each other.

Authentication is the process of verifying the identity of a user or system, ensuring that the requester has the necessary permissions to access a particular resource or perform specific actions.

In the context of APIs, authentication is crucial for maintaining the security and integrity of the services and data they expose.

Without proper authentication mechanisms, APIs would be vulnerable to unauthorized access, potentially leading to data breaches, misuse, and other security issues.

There are various methods and techniques used for API authentication, each with its strengths and weaknesses.

One of the most common authentication methods is API key-based authentication.

In this approach, the API provider issues a unique API key to each authorized user or application.

This key is typically included in the API request headers or as a query parameter when making requests to the API.

The API server checks the validity of the key and authorizes or denies access accordingly.

API key-based authentication is simple to implement and suitable for scenarios where the API consumers are trusted and can keep their keys secure.

However, it may not be the most secure option for high-risk applications or when dealing with untrusted clients since API keys can be exposed or compromised.

Another widely used authentication method is OAuth (Open Authorization).

OAuth is an open standard that allows applications to securely access resources on behalf of users.

It is commonly used in scenarios where third-party applications need to access a user's data, such as social media logins or connecting services like Google or Facebook to other applications.

OAuth involves the exchange of tokens, including access tokens and refresh tokens, to grant limited access to specific resources.

Access tokens are short-lived and provide temporary access to the user's data, while refresh tokens are used to obtain new access tokens without requiring the user to re-enter their credentials.

OAuth 2.0, the most recent version of OAuth, is widely adopted and provides a robust framework for secure authentication and authorization.

Bearer tokens are another form of API authentication, commonly used in conjunction with OAuth.

A bearer token is a cryptographic token that is included in API requests to prove the request's authenticity.

However, bearer tokens must be handled with care, as they provide access to the associated resources without further verification, making them vulnerable if exposed.

To enhance security, it's essential to use HTTPS (Hypertext Transfer Protocol Secure) to protect API communication, preventing eavesdropping and man-in-the-middle attacks.

Additionally, token validation and revocation mechanisms should be in place to detect and respond to compromised tokens promptly.

HTTP Basic Authentication is another straightforward API authentication method.

It involves sending a username and password with each API request, typically in the form of a base64-encoded string.

While this method is relatively simple to implement, it's essential to use it only with HTTPS to prevent exposing credentials in transit.

Furthermore, the use of HTTP Basic Authentication is declining in favor of more secure and flexible methods like OAuth.

Token-based authentication is gaining popularity due to its effectiveness and security.

In this approach, a token is issued to an authenticated user or application and must be included in subsequent API requests.

The token can be a JSON Web Token (JWT), which contains user or application information and is digitally signed to prevent tampering.

Token-based authentication allows for fine-grained control over access permissions and can be easily integrated with Single Sign-On (SSO) solutions.

One of the key benefits of token-based authentication is that it does not require the API server to maintain session state, making it scalable and suitable for distributed systems.

API authentication should also consider user authentication and authorization.

User authentication verifies the identity of a user, often requiring the user to provide a username and password or use a third-party authentication provider like Google or Facebook.

Once authenticated, the user's identity can be associated with specific roles or permissions to control what actions they can perform within the application or API.

Authorization determines whether a user or application has the necessary permissions to access a particular resource or perform a specific action.

Role-based access control (RBAC) and attribute-based access control (ABAC) are common methods for managing authorization in APIs.

RBAC assigns users or applications to predefined roles with associated permissions, while ABAC evaluates access decisions based on attributes like user attributes, resource attributes, and environmental conditions.

Implementing robust authentication and authorization mechanisms in APIs requires careful planning and consideration of security best practices.

It's essential to keep sensitive information like API keys, tokens, and user credentials secure.

Storing passwords securely, such as through hashing and salting, is crucial to prevent data breaches in the event of a security breach.

APIs should also implement rate limiting, which restricts the number of requests a user or application can make within a specific time frame.

Rate limiting helps prevent abuse and ensures fair resource allocation.

In addition to authentication and authorization, API security encompasses other aspects, such as input validation, data encryption, and monitoring for anomalies and potential attacks.

Regular security audits and penetration testing can help identify vulnerabilities and weaknesses in API implementations.

API documentation should include clear instructions on how to authenticate and use the API securely.

To summarize, understanding API authentication is vital for securing modern web services and ensuring that only authorized users or applications can access resources and perform actions.

There are various authentication methods, including API key-based authentication, OAuth, bearer tokens, and token-based authentication, each with its strengths and use cases.

User authentication and authorization are critical components of API security, and robust measures should be in place to protect sensitive data and resources.

Implementing secure API practices, including rate limiting, input validation, and encryption, is essential to protect against security threats and data breaches.

By following best practices and staying informed about emerging security threats, developers and organizations can build and maintain secure APIs that provide reliable and protected access to valuable resources.

Understanding and assessing API authorization mechanisms is crucial in ensuring the security of modern software systems.

API authorization determines what actions a user or application can perform within an application or service after they have been authenticated.

While authentication verifies the identity of the requester, authorization controls their access to specific resources and functionalities.

Assessing API authorization mechanisms involves evaluating the methods and techniques used to enforce access control and make informed decisions about whether they meet the security and business requirements.

One of the fundamental concepts in API authorization is access control.

Access control determines who can access a particular resource, such as a file, database record, or API endpoint, and what operations they can perform on it.

Effective access control mechanisms ensure that only authorized entities can access and modify resources, preventing unauthorized users or applications from gaining access.

There are several common approaches to API authorization, each with its strengths and considerations.

Role-Based Access Control (RBAC) is one of the most widely used authorization mechanisms.

In RBAC, users or applications are assigned specific roles, and each role is associated with a set of permissions or privileges.

These permissions define what actions a user or application with a particular role can perform within the system.

RBAC simplifies authorization management by grouping users or applications based on their responsibilities and access needs.

However, RBAC may not be fine-grained enough for complex authorization requirements or situations where access control needs to be based on attributes beyond user roles. Attribute-Based Access Control (ABAC) is another authorization model that offers more flexibility. ABAC makes access control decisions based on attributes, such as user attributes, resource attributes, and environmental conditions.

This approach allows for fine-grained access control by considering various contextual factors.

For example, an API could use ABAC to grant access to specific resources based on the user's department, location, or the time of day.

ABAC is particularly useful in scenarios where access control rules need to adapt to changing conditions.

Next, we have Rule-Based Access Control (RuBAC), which involves defining authorization rules that specify under what conditions access should be granted or denied.

These rules can be created using a policy language or rules engine that evaluates conditions and actions.

RuBAC offers considerable flexibility in defining access control logic but can become complex to manage as the number of rules grows.

In some cases, RuBAC may be used in conjunction with RBAC or ABAC to provide additional control.

Another important concept in API authorization is the principle of least privilege (PoLP).

The PoLP suggests that entities should be granted the minimum level of access required to perform their tasks, reducing the risk of privilege escalation and unauthorized access.

Implementing the PoLP ensures that users or applications do not have unnecessary permissions, limiting the potential impact of a security breach.

When assessing API authorization mechanisms, it's essential to consider various factors, including the sensitivity of the data and resources being protected.

Highly sensitive data may require more stringent authorization rules and stronger security measures.

Additionally, the volume of users or applications accessing the API and their specific roles should be considered when designing authorization policies.

API providers should also consider the potential impact of authorization failures.

For example, if an unauthorized user gains access to sensitive data, it could result in data breaches, compliance violations, and reputational damage.

Therefore, thorough testing and validation of authorization mechanisms are critical.

Security testing techniques, such as penetration testing and vulnerability scanning, can help identify weaknesses in authorization controls.

In addition to these traditional methods, API providers should consider incorporating automated authorization testing into their development and testing processes.

Tools and libraries designed for testing authorization flows can help identify vulnerabilities and misconfigurations.

Furthermore, API documentation should include clear guidelines for implementing and configuring authorization.

API consumers need to understand how to request and use the necessary permissions effectively.

Another essential aspect of API authorization assessment is monitoring and auditing.

Logging access control decisions, failed authorization attempts, and changes to authorization policies allows organizations to detect and respond to security incidents and policy violations.

Continuous monitoring can help identify suspicious or abnormal access patterns, potentially indicating unauthorized access attempts or insider threats.

Finally, organizations should regularly review and update their authorization policies to adapt to changing business requirements and security threats.

Policy reviews should involve key stakeholders, including security teams, developers, and business analysts, to ensure that authorization rules align with organizational goals.

In summary, assessing API authorization mechanisms is a critical aspect of API security.

Effective authorization controls are essential for protecting sensitive data and resources from unauthorized access.

Different authorization models, such as RBAC, ABAC, and RuBAC, offer varying levels of flexibility and control.

Consideration should be given to the principle of least privilege and the potential impact of authorization failures.

Thorough testing, monitoring, and auditing are essential for identifying and addressing vulnerabilities in authorization mechanisms.

Regular policy reviews and updates ensure that access control rules remain aligned with organizational requirements and security best practices.

Chapter 7: Web Application Firewalls (WAFs) Bypass Techniques

Evading Web Application Firewall (WAF) detection is a topic of significant interest for security researchers and attackers alike.

A Web Application Firewall is a security solution that is designed to protect web applications from a variety of attacks, including SQL injection, cross-site scripting (XSS), and cross-site request forgery (CSRF).

WAFs analyze incoming HTTP requests to detect and block malicious traffic before it can reach the web application.

However, attackers are continually developing new techniques to evade WAF detection and carry out attacks.

Understanding these evasion techniques is essential for both defenders and security professionals to better protect web applications.

One common method used to evade WAF detection is obfuscation.

Attackers can obfuscate malicious payloads by encoding or encrypting them in various ways to make them appear benign to the WAF.

For example, base64 encoding can be used to obfuscate SQL injection payloads, making them harder to detect.

Furthermore, attackers may employ different character encoding schemes or escape sequences to bypass signature-based detection.

Another evasion technique is the use of alternative HTTP methods.

WAFs often focus on detecting malicious payloads in commonly used HTTP methods like GET and POST.

Attackers can evade detection by using less common methods such as PUT, DELETE, or OPTIONS to inject malicious payloads.

WAFs may not inspect these less frequently used methods as closely, providing attackers with an opportunity to bypass detection.

The manipulation of HTTP headers is another tactic employed by attackers to evade WAFs.

By modifying or adding HTTP headers to their requests, attackers can hide malicious intent or make the traffic appear legitimate.

For instance, they may manipulate the Referer header or User-Agent header to deceive the WAF.

Another evasion technique is payload fragmentation, where attackers split malicious payloads into smaller, less detectable parts.

This fragmentation can confuse the WAF, which may not recognize the malicious intent when the payload is distributed across multiple requests.

Additionally, attackers may use HTTP request smuggling, a more advanced evasion technique.

HTTP request smuggling takes advantage of discrepancies in how different components of a web application stack process and interpret HTTP requests.

By carefully crafting requests that exploit these discrepancies, attackers can bypass WAFs and gain unauthorized access.

To protect against evasion techniques, organizations should implement a combination of security measures.

One approach is to use a Web Application Firewall that is regularly updated with the latest threat intelligence and signatures.

This helps ensure that the WAF can detect and block the most recent evasion techniques.

Implementing strict input validation and output encoding in the web application's code can also help mitigate the risk of attacks.

By validating and sanitizing user input and encoding output, organizations can prevent many common attack vectors.

Furthermore, the use of intrusion detection systems (IDS) and intrusion prevention systems (IPS) in conjunction with WAFs can provide an additional layer of security.

IDS and IPS solutions can monitor network traffic and detect suspicious patterns or anomalies, complementing the WAF's capabilities.

Regularly auditing and testing web applications for security vulnerabilities, including evasion techniques, is essential.

Penetration testing and vulnerability scanning can help identify weaknesses in the application's defenses.

Security professionals should be aware of the latest evasion techniques and stay informed about emerging threats through security communities and resources.

Additionally, organizations should adopt a proactive security posture, focusing on threat modeling and risk assessments to identify potential weaknesses and address them before they can be exploited.

In summary, evading Web Application Firewall detection is a persistent challenge in the field of cybersecurity.

Attackers continue to develop new evasion techniques to bypass WAFs and carry out attacks on web applications.

Understanding these techniques and implementing robust security measures is crucial for organizations to protect their web applications from malicious actors.

By staying informed, regularly testing for vulnerabilities, and employing a combination of security solutions, organizations can better defend against evasion attempts and enhance their overall security posture.

Exploiting SQL injection vulnerabilities is a topic that lies at the intersection of cybersecurity and database management.

SQL injection is a type of attack that targets web applications by manipulating the SQL queries sent to the underlying database.

It is a prevalent and potentially devastating attack vector that can lead to unauthorized access, data theft, or even complete compromise of a web application.

Understanding how SQL injection works and how to exploit these vulnerabilities is crucial for both security professionals and developers to protect their applications effectively.

SQL injection occurs when an attacker can inject malicious SQL code into an application's input fields.

These input fields often interact with a web application's database, and if not properly sanitized or validated, they can be used to execute arbitrary SQL commands.

One common form of SQL injection is known as "classic" or "union-based" SQL injection.

In this type of attack, the attacker inserts malicious SQL statements into input fields, attempting to manipulate the SQL query executed by the application.

For example, they may input something like "1' UNION SELECT username, password FROM users--" into a login form.

If the application is vulnerable, this input can result in a SQL query that combines the user-supplied input with the query used for authentication, effectively granting the attacker access to the user credentials.

Another variant of SQL injection is "blind" SQL injection, where the attacker does not receive direct feedback from the application.

Instead, they craft SQL queries in a way that relies on the application's response, such as a true or false condition.

By repeatedly manipulating the input and observing the application's behavior, attackers can deduce information about the database's structure and content.

Time-based blind SQL injection is one example where attackers induce a delay in the application's response to determine if their injected query is true or false.

Error-based SQL injection is another variant where attackers intentionally trigger database errors to gather information about the database schema or contents.

To exploit SQL injection vulnerabilities successfully, attackers often rely on a combination of techniques.

They may use automated tools like SQLMap or manually craft payloads to test input fields systematically.

It's essential for security professionals to understand these attack methods to prevent them effectively.

One common defense against SQL injection is input validation and parameterized queries.

Developers should validate and sanitize user input and use prepared statements or parameterized queries to interact with the database.

This ensures that user input is treated as data, not executable code.

Additionally, implementing proper authentication and authorization mechanisms can limit the potential impact of SQL injection attacks.

Role-based access controls and the principle of least privilege should guide access to sensitive database resources.

Web application firewalls (WAFs) can also provide protection against SQL injection by filtering and blocking malicious requests.

Regular security testing, including penetration testing and code reviews, is crucial for identifying and addressing SQL injection vulnerabilities in web applications.

Security professionals can use tools and manual testing techniques to discover and remediate these issues.

In summary, exploiting SQL injection vulnerabilities is a critical concern for web application security.

Attackers leverage various techniques to manipulate SQL queries and gain unauthorized access to databases.

Understanding the types of SQL injection attacks and their methods is essential for security professionals and developers.

Implementing best practices, such as input validation, parameterized queries, and regular security testing, can help mitigate the risks associated with SQL injection and protect web applications from these pervasive threats.

Chapter 8: Exploiting Common Web App Vulnerabilities

Taking advantage of Cross-Site Request Forgery (CSRF) is a topic that delves into the realm of web application security.

CSRF is a type of web vulnerability that can have serious consequences if not properly addressed.

Understanding how CSRF attacks work and how to exploit them is essential for security professionals and developers to protect web applications effectively.

A CSRF attack occurs when an attacker tricks a user into performing actions on a web application without their consent.

The attacker crafts a malicious request, such as changing the user's password or making a financial transaction, and then persuades the victim to unwittingly execute this request.

One way to exploit CSRF is to embed malicious code or links within web content, such as a website, email, or forum post, that the victim accesses.

When the victim visits the compromised page or interacts with the malicious content, their browser sends authenticated requests to the target web application, performing actions on behalf of the victim.

The attacker's goal is to leverage the victim's authenticated session to execute unauthorized actions.

To illustrate this, imagine a scenario where a user is logged into their online banking account in one browser tab while browsing another website in a different tab.

An attacker sends the victim a link to a website containing a hidden, malicious request that triggers a fund transfer from the victim's bank account.

If the victim clicks on the link while logged into their bank account, their session is used to execute the malicious transfer without their knowledge.

Another way to exploit CSRF is through malicious forms embedded in a website.

The attacker creates a form that performs actions on a target website, such as changing account settings, and tricks the victim into submitting this form.

When the victim submits the form, the actions specified within it are carried out using the victim's authenticated session.

To mitigate the risk of CSRF attacks, web developers can implement measures like using anti-CSRF tokens.

These tokens are unique, random values generated for each user session.

They are included in forms and requests, and the web application checks whether the token provided by the client matches the expected value.

If not, the request is rejected.

This approach prevents attackers from crafting malicious requests because they would not possess the correct anti-CSRF token.

To exploit CSRF vulnerabilities successfully, attackers must find ways to trick users into unknowingly executing malicious requests.

They often rely on social engineering tactics to persuade victims to click on links or submit forms.

For example, they may disguise malicious links as harmless ones or use enticing language to encourage users to take action.

Furthermore, attackers may utilize techniques like URL shorteners or URL obfuscation to make malicious links less suspicious.

Attackers also consider the timing of their attacks, often seeking to exploit vulnerabilities when victims are more likely to be logged into targeted web applications.

For instance, they might time their attacks to coincide with peak user activity, such as during online shopping seasons or major events.

Another technique is to combine CSRF attacks with other vulnerabilities.

For instance, an attacker might discover a CSRF vulnerability in an application and then use it in conjunction with a stored cross-site scripting (XSS) vulnerability to create a more convincing attack.

Security professionals should be aware of these tactics to better defend against CSRF attacks.

Protecting against CSRF involves implementing security mechanisms like anti-CSRF tokens, validating and sanitizing user input, and educating users about potential threats.

Additionally, web application security testing, including manual testing and automated scanning, can help identify and remediate CSRF vulnerabilities.

In summary, taking advantage of Cross-Site Request Forgery (CSRF) is a complex and potentially harmful attack vector in web application security.

Attackers exploit users' authenticated sessions to perform unauthorized actions on their behalf.

Understanding how CSRF attacks work and the methods attackers use is essential for security professionals and developers to effectively defend against these threats.

Implementing countermeasures like anti-CSRF tokens and user education can help protect web applications and their users from CSRF attacks.

Session hijacking and cookie manipulation are critical topics in the field of cybersecurity, as they pertain to the unauthorized takeover of user sessions and the manipulation of cookies in web applications.

Web applications often use cookies to store session identifiers, which help maintain user sessions after authentication.

These cookies contain sensitive information, including session tokens, user IDs, and authentication credentials.

Session hijacking, also known as session fixation, is an attack where an unauthorized user gains control of another user's session.

The attacker can then impersonate the victim and perform actions on the web application as if they were the legitimate user.

To understand session hijacking, it's important to grasp how web applications manage user sessions.

When a user logs into a web application, the server generates a session identifier or token, which is unique for that session.

This identifier is often stored in a cookie on the user's device and is sent with every subsequent request to the application.

The server uses this token to associate the user with their session data, allowing them to navigate the application without repeatedly logging in.

Now, imagine an attacker intercepting this session token.

There are several ways an attacker can hijack a session.

One common method is through session fixation, where the attacker sets the victim's session token to a known value.

This can be achieved by tricking the victim into clicking on a link or visiting a website controlled by the attacker.

Once the victim logs in, their session token is set to the value chosen by the attacker, effectively granting them control over the victim's session.

Another technique is session interception, where the attacker captures the victim's session token during its transmission.

This can occur on unsecured public Wi-Fi networks or when using insecure communication channels.

If an attacker can eavesdrop on the victim's network traffic, they may capture the session token as it is sent from the user's device to the server.

Session fixation and session interception are serious security threats, and web developers must implement countermeasures to mitigate them.

One common defense mechanism is the use of secure cookies.

Secure cookies can only be transmitted over secure (HTTPS) connections, making it difficult for attackers to intercept them.

Additionally, developers should regularly rotate session tokens, invalidate old ones after logout, and implement session timeout mechanisms to reduce the window of opportunity for session hijacking.

Cookie manipulation is another attack vector that overlaps with session hijacking.

Cookies are used to store various types of data, including user preferences, shopping cart contents, and authentication information.

Malicious actors can manipulate cookies to alter their content or exploit vulnerabilities in cookie processing.

For example, an attacker may manipulate a cookie's value to gain unauthorized access to an account.

They might change the user's role, alter their access permissions, or modify the contents of the shopping cart.

To mitigate cookie manipulation, developers should validate and sanitize cookie data on the server-side, ensuring that it matches expected values and hasn't been tampered with.

Additionally, implementing secure coding practices and conducting regular security audits can help identify and remediate potential vulnerabilities in cookie handling.

In both session hijacking and cookie manipulation scenarios, security awareness and user education play crucial roles.

Users should be cautious about clicking on links from untrusted sources and avoid using public Wi-Fi networks for sensitive transactions whenever possible.

Educating users about the risks of session hijacking and cookie manipulation can help them make informed decisions and protect themselves online.

Furthermore, organizations should consider implementing multi-factor authentication (MFA) to add an extra layer of security to user accounts.

MFA requires users to provide two or more forms of identification before gaining access, making it more challenging for attackers to hijack sessions even if they have the session token.

Another strategy to combat session hijacking is the use of token-based authentication systems.

These systems rely on short-lived tokens instead of traditional cookies to authenticate users.

Tokens are generated on the server and issued to the client, typically stored in local storage or a session storage, rather than in cookies.

Tokens are less susceptible to session hijacking because they are not automatically sent with every HTTP request, reducing the attack surface.

Additionally, tokens can be designed to have limited lifetimes, further enhancing security.

In summary, session hijacking and cookie manipulation are significant threats to the security of web applications and user data.

Understanding the mechanics of these attacks, as well as implementing strong security measures, is essential to protect against them.

Developers must adopt secure coding practices, employ encryption and secure cookies, and educate users to minimize the risks associated with session hijacking and cookie manipulation.

By taking these steps, organizations can better safeguard their web applications and user accounts from these pervasive security threats.

Chapter 9: Advanced Session Management and Authentication Attacks

Authentication is a critical aspect of computer security, serving as the gatekeeper that verifies the identity of users and grants them access to systems, applications, or data.

Authentication methods typically involve something the user knows, such as a password, something the user has, like a smart card, or something inherent to the user, such as biometrics.

However, even with robust authentication mechanisms in place, vulnerabilities and techniques exist that can potentially bypass or subvert these safeguards.

One common authentication bypass technique is password guessing, where an attacker attempts to gain access to an account by systematically trying different passwords until they find the correct one.

This technique is often automated using password cracking tools that leverage dictionaries, brute-force attacks, or previously breached password databases.

To mitigate password guessing attacks, organizations should enforce strong password policies, encourage the use of multi-factor authentication (MFA), and implement account lockout mechanisms after a certain number of failed login attempts.

Another authentication bypass method is credential stuffing, where attackers use known username and password combinations obtained from previous data breaches to gain unauthorized access to other online accounts.

Since many people reuse passwords across multiple sites and services, attackers can exploit this behavior to compromise accounts.

To protect against credential stuffing attacks, users should be educated about the risks of password reuse and the importance of using unique passwords for different accounts.

Implementing MFA is also an effective countermeasure, as it adds an additional layer of security that is difficult for attackers to overcome.

Phishing attacks represent another way to bypass authentication.

In a phishing attack, an attacker typically sends fraudulent emails or messages that appear to come from a legitimate source, such as a bank or a well-known online service.

These messages often contain links to fake login pages designed to capture users' login credentials when they unwittingly enter them.

By tricking users into revealing their login information, attackers can gain access to accounts without directly attacking the authentication system.

To combat phishing attacks, organizations should educate their employees and users about recognizing phishing attempts and promote the use of security awareness training.

Email filtering and web filtering tools can also help detect and block phishing emails and malicious websites.

In addition to password guessing, credential stuffing, and phishing, there are other authentication bypass techniques that rely on software vulnerabilities and weaknesses.

One such technique is exploiting insecure authentication protocols.

Outdated and weak authentication protocols can expose systems to attacks that allow attackers to bypass authentication entirely.

Organizations should regularly update and patch their software to ensure that secure authentication protocols are in use.

Similarly, attackers may take advantage of vulnerabilities in the authentication process itself, such as session fixation or race conditions, to bypass authentication.

Security assessments and penetration testing can help identify and address such vulnerabilities in an organization's systems and applications.

Another technique used to bypass authentication is session hijacking, where an attacker intercepts or steals a user's session token to gain unauthorized access to their account.

This often occurs when session tokens are not adequately protected or are exposed through insecure channels.

Implementing secure session management practices, such as securing session tokens and using secure cookies, can help prevent session hijacking.

An advanced authentication bypass technique involves exploiting flaws in single sign-on (SSO) implementations.

SSO allows users to access multiple applications with a single set of credentials, making it a valuable target for attackers.

Weaknesses in SSO implementations can be leveraged to bypass authentication and gain access to multiple systems.

To protect against SSO-related authentication bypass, organizations should perform regular security assessments of their SSO infrastructure and follow best practices for SSO configuration.

Another sophisticated technique is time-based attacks, which exploit timing vulnerabilities in authentication systems.

By measuring the time it takes for an authentication system to respond to different inputs, attackers can deduce valuable information about the authentication process and potentially find weaknesses.

To defend against time-based attacks, organizations should implement consistent and constant timing in their authentication processes.

In summary, authentication bypass techniques represent a significant challenge in the field of cybersecurity.

While there are various methods that attackers may employ to bypass authentication, organizations and users can take proactive steps to protect their systems and data. These steps include strong password policies, multi-factor authentication, security awareness training, regular software updates and patching, secure session management, and robust single sign-on configurations.

By staying vigilant and implementing effective security measures, individuals and organizations can reduce the risk of falling victim to authentication bypass attacks and enhance their overall cybersecurity posture.

Chapter 10: Reporting and Remediation in Web App Scanning

Documenting vulnerabilities and exploits is a crucial aspect of the cybersecurity field, as it plays a pivotal role in understanding, mitigating, and preventing security threats.

When security professionals discover vulnerabilities in software, hardware, or systems, it's essential to document these findings in a comprehensive and organized manner.

Documentation serves several essential purposes, such as providing a detailed record of the vulnerability, its potential impact, and the steps to reproduce it.

By documenting vulnerabilities thoroughly, security teams can ensure that all necessary information is available for analysis and remediation.

One key element of documenting vulnerabilities is accurately describing the nature of the security flaw.

This includes identifying the affected software or hardware, specifying the version or configuration where the vulnerability exists, and detailing the steps to replicate the issue.

Precise and clear descriptions enable other security professionals to understand the problem quickly and determine its severity.

In addition to the technical aspects, documenting vulnerabilities should include information about the potential impact of the flaw.

This involves assessing the potential consequences of a successful exploitation, such as unauthorized access, data leaks, or service disruptions.

Understanding the impact helps organizations prioritize which vulnerabilities to address first.

Moreover, documentation should include information about the severity of the vulnerability.

Various systems use different rating systems, such as the Common Vulnerability Scoring System (CVSS), to assign severity scores based on factors like exploitability and impact.

These scores provide a standardized way to assess and prioritize vulnerabilities.

Furthermore, documenting vulnerabilities should include any known remediation or mitigation steps.

This information is crucial for organizations to take immediate actions to protect their systems while waiting for vendor-provided patches or updates.

If a temporary workaround exists, it should be clearly documented to help organizations minimize the risk until a permanent fix is available.

In some cases, a security professional may discover a zero-day vulnerability, which is a security flaw that is unknown to the vendor and has no available patch.

Documenting zero-day vulnerabilities is particularly important because they present a significant risk.

Security researchers must carefully document the zero-day vulnerability, including its technical details, potential impact, and any countermeasures or mitigations that can be applied until a patch becomes available.

Sharing this information responsibly with relevant parties, such as the affected vendor or a trusted security coordination center, is critical to ensure the issue is addressed promptly without causing widespread harm.

Aside from vulnerabilities, documenting exploits is another essential aspect of cybersecurity.

An exploit is a piece of code or a sequence of actions that takes advantage of a vulnerability to compromise a system or application.

Security professionals may develop exploits for various reasons, including demonstrating the impact of a vulnerability, testing defenses, or validating the effectiveness of a patch.

Documenting exploits involves recording the code or techniques used to leverage a vulnerability.

This documentation is essential for understanding how an attacker could potentially abuse the vulnerability and for developing appropriate defenses.

Security researchers often create proof-of-concept (PoC) exploits to demonstrate the feasibility and impact of an attack.

A PoC exploit is a concrete example of how a vulnerability can be exploited, which helps others, including vendors and defenders, understand the risk better.

When documenting PoC exploits, researchers should provide step-by-step instructions and code snippets to enable others to replicate the exploit.

It's crucial to strike a balance between providing enough information for educational purposes and avoiding publishing overly detailed information that could be misused by malicious actors.

In addition to the technical details of an exploit, documentation should include information about potential mitigations and countermeasures.

For instance, if an exploit targets a specific software version, the documentation should recommend upgrading to a patched version or applying other protective measures.

Security professionals who discover or develop exploits often follow responsible disclosure practices.

Responsible disclosure involves reporting the vulnerability and the associated exploit details to the affected vendor or organization before publicly sharing the information.

This approach allows the vendor to develop and release a patch or mitigation strategy to protect users before malicious actors can take advantage of the vulnerability.

In cases where vendors are unresponsive or unwilling to address the issue, some security researchers may opt for full disclosure, making all details about the vulnerability and exploit public.

However, responsible disclosure is generally preferred to minimize the risk to users and organizations.

Documenting vulnerabilities and exploits is also essential for maintaining an accurate and up-to-date inventory of security threats.

Security teams can use this documentation to track the status of vulnerabilities, prioritize remediation efforts, and ensure that all known security issues are addressed in a timely manner.

Moreover, organizations can use documented vulnerabilities and exploits to inform risk assessments and compliance efforts.

By maintaining a comprehensive record of security weaknesses and their potential impact, organizations can demonstrate due diligence in addressing cybersecurity threats.

In summary, documenting vulnerabilities and exploits is a fundamental practice in the field of cybersecurity.

It involves accurately describing security flaws, assessing their impact and severity, and providing guidance on remediation and mitigation.

Documentation plays a critical role in responsible disclosure, risk management, and maintaining an effective security posture.

Security professionals must ensure that their documentation is clear, informative, and securely managed to protect sensitive information and minimize the risk of exploitation.

Prioritizing and executing remediation actions is a critical aspect of managing cybersecurity risks and ensuring the security of an organization's digital assets. When a security vulnerability or weakness is identified within an organization's systems, applications, or network infrastructure, it's essential to take prompt and well-considered actions to address the issue effectively.

The process of prioritizing and executing remediation actions begins with the identification of vulnerabilities and weaknesses. These vulnerabilities can be discovered through various means, such as regular security assessments, vulnerability scans, penetration testing, or incident response activities. It's crucial to have a well-defined and documented process for reporting and documenting vulnerabilities as they are identified.

Once vulnerabilities are identified, they must be assessed and prioritized based on their severity and potential impact. Severity assessments are often guided by industry-standard frameworks like the Common

Vulnerability Scoring System (CVSS), which assigns a score to each vulnerability based on factors such as exploitability and impact. Vulnerabilities with higher scores are generally considered more severe and require more immediate attention.

In addition to the CVSS score, the potential impact of a vulnerability must be considered. This involves evaluating what an attacker could achieve if they successfully exploit the vulnerability. For example, a critical vulnerability in a web server that could lead to remote code execution may have a higher impact than a low-severity vulnerability that only allows for information disclosure.

Once vulnerabilities are assessed and prioritized, organizations can develop a remediation plan. This plan outlines the specific steps and actions required to mitigate or eliminate each identified vulnerability. Remediation actions can vary widely and may include applying security patches, updating software or configurations, implementing access controls, or modifying network settings.

The prioritization of vulnerabilities in the remediation plan is critical, as it ensures that the most severe and impactful vulnerabilities are addressed first. This helps organizations focus their resources and efforts on reducing the most significant security risks.

In some cases, vulnerabilities may have well-documented vendor-provided patches or updates. In these instances, organizations can follow established procedures to apply these fixes. However, applying patches is not always straightforward, as it may require testing in a controlled environment to ensure that they do not introduce new issues or disrupt existing systems.

In cases where no vendor-provided patch is available, organizations may need to implement other mitigations or workarounds to reduce the risk associated with the vulnerability. These measures can include adjusting firewall rules, disabling vulnerable services, or implementing intrusion detection and prevention systems to detect and block exploitation attempts.

Another important aspect of executing remediation actions is change management. Any changes made to an organization's systems or network must be carefully documented, tested, and approved before implementation. Change management processes help ensure that remediation actions are carried out without introducing unintended consequences or vulnerabilities.

Effective communication is also vital during the remediation process. Stakeholders within the organization, including IT teams, security teams, and management, should be informed about the status of remediation efforts. Timely and transparent communication helps build awareness of the security risks and the progress being made to address them.

Once remediation actions have been executed, it's essential to verify their effectiveness. This often involves retesting systems or applications to confirm that the vulnerabilities have been successfully mitigated. In some cases, third-party security assessments or penetration testing may be employed to validate the security posture of an organization after remediation.

Ongoing monitoring and continuous improvement are critical aspects of the remediation process. Cybersecurity threats and vulnerabilities are constantly evolving, so organizations must remain vigilant and proactive in their efforts to identify and address new risks. Regular security assessments and vulnerability scanning are essential to detect emerging threats and vulnerabilities.

In some cases, organizations may choose to implement compensating controls if immediate remediation is not possible. Compensating controls are security measures that are put in place to mitigate the risk associated with a vulnerability until a permanent fix can be implemented. These controls may include enhanced monitoring, network segmentation, or additional security layers.

The prioritization and execution of remediation actions should align with an organization's overall risk management strategy. This strategy considers the organization's risk tolerance, business objectives, and compliance requirements. Remediation efforts should be directed towards reducing the most critical risks that have the potential to impact the organization's core business functions and data assets.

In summary, prioritizing and executing remediation actions is a vital component of an organization's cybersecurity strategy. It involves identifying, assessing, and addressing vulnerabilities and weaknesses in a systematic and risk-based manner. Effective remediation efforts help protect an organization's digital assets, reduce security risks, and ensure the continued integrity and availability of critical systems and data.

Conclusion

In this comprehensive book bundle, "Red Team Operations: Attack," we have delved deep into the world of cybersecurity, ethical hacking, and the strategies employed by red team professionals to identify and mitigate vulnerabilities. Across four insightful books, we've explored the essential skills and tactics needed to simulate real-world attacks and strengthen an organization's security posture.

In "Book 1 - Red Team Essentials: A Beginner's Guide to Attack Strategies," we laid the foundation for understanding the fundamentals of red teaming, emphasizing the importance of planning, reconnaissance, and attack methodologies. We introduced readers to the mindset and techniques required to emulate adversaries effectively.

Moving on to "Book 2 - Unlocking the Black Box: Advanced Techniques in Ethical Hacking," we took a deeper dive into the world of ethical hacking. We explored advanced penetration testing and vulnerability assessment techniques, equipping readers with the knowledge to uncover hidden weaknesses within systems and applications.

"Book 3 - Mastering the Art of Social Engineering: Tactics for Red Team Professionals" delved into the human element of security. We explored the psychology behind social engineering and the strategies used by attackers to manipulate individuals. Readers gained insights into the tactics employed by red team professionals to raise awareness and protect against social engineering attacks.

Finally, in "Book 4 - Web App Scanning Mastery: Expert Techniques for Red Team Specialists," we explored the realm of web application security. From scanning and vulnerability assessment to understanding API authentication and evading WAF detection, readers learned how to identify and exploit vulnerabilities in web applications, a critical skill in modern cybersecurity. Throughout this bundle, we've emphasized the importance of responsible and ethical hacking practices. Our goal has been to equip readers with the knowledge and tools needed to strengthen cybersecurity defenses and protect against real-world threats. By mastering the art of red teaming, ethical hacking, social engineering, and web application security, readers are better prepared to face the ever-evolving landscape of cyber threats.

As we conclude this journey through "Red Team Operations: Attack," we encourage readers to continue their pursuit of knowledge and expertise in the field of cybersecurity. The world of digital threats is constantly evolving, and staying ahead requires ongoing learning and adaptation. With the skills and insights gained from this bundle, readers are well-equipped to contribute to the ongoing battle for a secure digital world.

www.ingramcontent.com/pod-product-compliance
Lightning Source LLC
Chambersburg PA
CBHW071236050326
40690CB00011B/2142